Lewis Macnaughten Humbert

Memorials of the Hospital of St. Cross and Alms House of Noble

Poverty

Lewis Macnaughten Humbert

Memorials of the Hospital of St. Cross and Alms House of Noble Poverty

ISBN/EAN: 9783337092443

Printed in Europe, USA, Canada, Australia, Japan

Cover: Foto ©ninafisch / pixelio.de

More available books at **www.hansebooks.com**

MEMORIALS

OF THE

HOSPITAL OF ST. CROSS

AND

Alms House of Noble Poverty.

BY THE

REV. L. M. HUMBERT,

M.A. OF ST. JOHN'S COLLEGE, OXFORD, AND
MASTER OF ST. CROSS.

ILLUSTRATED WITH THIRTEEN PHOTOGRAPHS BY W. SAVAGE,
AND NUMEROUS WOODCUTS.

WINCHESTER:

WILLIAM SAVAGE, PHOTOGRAPHIC PUBLISHER, HIGH STREET.

LONDON:

MESSRS. PARKER & CO., 377, STRAND.

MDCCCLXVIII.

To the Right Reverend

Charles Richard Sumner, D.D.,

Lord Bishop of Winchester;
Prelate of the most noble Order of the Garter;
Patron and Visitor of the Hospital of Saint Cross.

My Lord,

With deep thankfulness I avail myself of the privilege of sending forth these pages under your Lordship's patronage. Whether from a public or private point of view, there is assuredly no one to whom I could with so much propriety dedicate these Memorials of St. Cross. Originally founded by one of your distinguished predecessors in the See of Winchester, resuscitated by another, and largely endowed by a third; this noble Institution is, in these last days, not a little indebted to your Lordship's own generous supervision.

The times of De Blois and Beaufort, of Wykeham and Fox, have long since passed away; and our lot is cast in days of retrenchment and economy. But we rejoice that the See of Winchester, (spared during your Lordship's Episcopate), has hitherto remained unimpaired; and that while we possess a spiritual Father in the Gospel, we have also a Prelate in whose large and unostentatious liberality we are often reminded of the munificence and zeal that distinguished some of the earlier rulers of this important diocese.

NOTHING could have elicited more strongly the expression of regard and filial affection entertained by your clergy than the recent serious illness with which it pleased God to visit your Lordship, to the sorrow of all classes alike, throughout your extensive jurisdiction. God has graciously heard the prayers offered up from so many hearts; and still preserves your valuable life, for the comfort of your family, the good of your diocese, and the welfare of the Church at large. That He may long continue to do so, and that we may long reap the benefit of your fatherly counsels, and gladly follow your godly admonitions, is the sincere prayer of the Master and Brethren of your Hospital of St. Cross.

I remain,

MY LORD,

With affectionate respect,

Your Lordship's faithful and devoted Servant,

L. M. HUMBERT.

July, 1868.

PREFACE.

IT will be scarcely deemed necessary to offer any apology to the Public, for the publication of a new and more complete Work descriptive of the past History, the present aspect, and the future prospects, of this unique Foundation. The graphic and faithful sketch of the historian MILNER belongs to a past era. Even the Lecture of the present MASTER, delivered nearly twelve years ago to the Hampshire Church School Society, though it has reached a fourth edition, can hardly satisfy the requirements of more than the passing stranger who visits the ancient place for an hour, and desires to carry away a brief and inexpensive reminiscence.

The present work is designed to supply what seems to be a real want. It not only offers an elegant appendage to the drawing room or library table; but, it is hoped, an acceptable and permanent contribution to the archæology of Hampshire; and with this view the MASTER intends to make as much use of the valuable Documents under his custody as may be consistent with what is meant to be a popular Work.

It must be added, that the Book has been projected in the hope of procuring, by means of its sale, further funds towards continuing the Restoration of the Church of St. Cross, which though so well begun, is still far from completed. Many remnants testify to the richness and character of the stained glass which once filled its windows: it is desired to devote the means which may become thus available *specifically* to the restoration of that portion of its former magnificence.

Unavoidable absence from home has somewhat limited the Author's opportunities of consulting manuscripts and memoranda, to which he could otherwise have had free access at all times; and a reference or verification not made at the moment is sometimes forgotten till too late. While, however, he ventures to plead this as some apology for any inaccuracy or omission which may have crept into his little book, and escaped detection on his part, he trusts that the work has not suffered materially from the cause thus named. He only hopes that the subject may prove one tithe as interesting to the reader, as it is to the writer, to whom its preparation has been truly a "labour of love."

CONTENTS.

Part One.

PAST HISTORY OF THE PLACE.

Part Two.

PRESENT ASPECT AND EXISTING BUILDINGS.

Part Three.

RESTORATION AND FUTURE PROSPECTS.

Index.

WOODCUTS FROM PHOTOGRAPHS AND SKETCHES BY MR. SAVAGE.

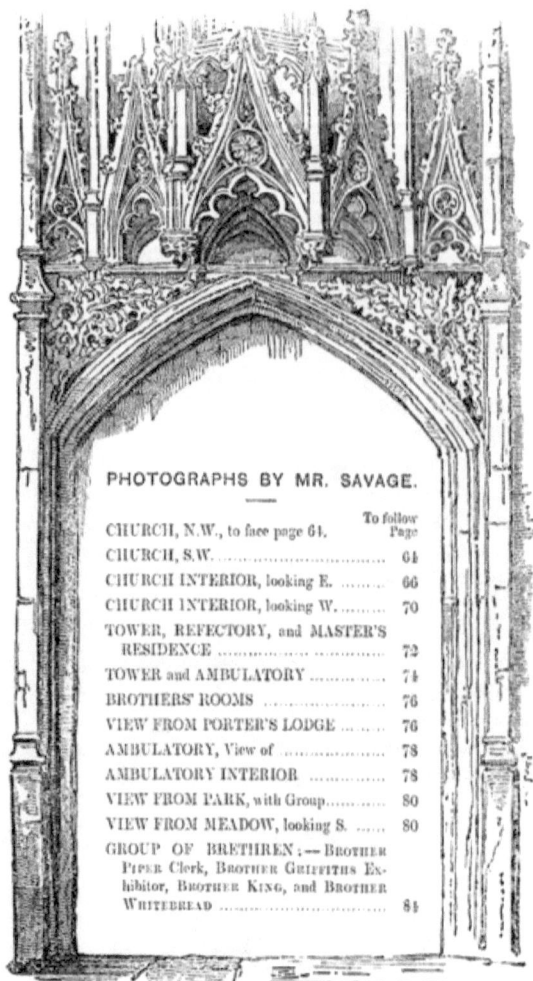

PHOTOGRAPHS BY MR. SAVAGE.

PART I.

Past History of the Place.

"HAIL! pious roofs, by grateful HENRY raised,
Where toil-worn age may rest, and Christ be praised!
The tidal sweep of time on kindred halls
Has scarcely left a remnant of their walls,
Save where that faithful friend to ruined things,
The mantling ivy timely succour brings,
And by her strong tough arms and hands sustains
The crumbling vestiges of what remains.
But thine, *St. Cross,* a kinder fate have found;
No ruins here deform thy hallowed ground;
Nor e'er has echo from thy towers been driven
Since first they rose and heard the song of heaven."

THERE are some Institutions and Buildings which so unmistakeably bear upon their surface and upon all their surroundings the aspect of antiquity that they seem to invite investigation; and to stand out as credible witnesses of bygone ages, waiting to be questioned and cross-examined as to the part they have borne, and the scenes they have witnessed, in times remote.

ST. CROSS will be recognised at first sight as one of these speaking monuments; and on further acquaintance and examination will not disappoint our just expectations. Its ancient charters and leases, registers and accounts, have been very fairly preserved; and little more than patient industry is required to construct a reliable narrative of its rise and progress, from the early days of our purely Norman Sovereigns to the present time.

We begin with its Foundation by DE BLOIS.

B

FOUNDATION BY HENRY DE BLOIS.

HENRY, the brother of King Stephen and grandson of the Conqueror, was promoted by his uncle, Henry I, from the Abbey of Glastonbury to the Episcopal See of Winchester, and consecrated in A.D. 1129. It appears that, even in earlier times than his, there had been a religious foundation upon the same spot, which had been left in ruins by the Danes. Of this, however, little or nothing is certainly known. The real history of St. Cross begins with the episcopate of DE BLOIS; and, as early as A.D. 1137, in the month of March, there is a Bull of Pope Innocent II confirming the rights and possessions of the Hospital. In May, A.D. 1144, Lucius II confirms the same more fully; specifying the names of several churches, including Fareham and Twyford, whose tithes were appropriated to the support of this charity, which was expressly founded for "the Poor of Christ, humbly and devoutly serving God."

The following is a translation of a portion of the Charter of Foundation. "The "manner of the service and the constitutions made by me are these:—Thirteen poor "men, feeble and so reduced in strength that they can scarcely, or not at all, support "themselves without other aid,* shall remain in the same Hospital constantly; to "whom necessary clothing, provided by the Prior of the Establishment, shall be "given, and beds fit for their infirmities; and daily a good loaf of wheaten bread of "the weight of five measures, three dishes at dinner, and one for supper, and drink "in sufficient quantity......And, besides these thirteen poor men, one hundred other "poor persons, as deserving as can be found and more indigent, shall be received at "the hour of dinner, &c......And other benefits also, to be mercifully performed to "those in need, we command to be done according to the ability of the House."

Such were the simple objects of the pious Founder of this place:—that the "poor of Christ" might be suitably clothed and fed; that they might have the opportunity of "humbly and devoutly serving God" in the sanctuary; and that, in proportion to the means in hand, other works of piety and mercy should be here

---

* "Ita viribus attenuati ut vix aut nunquam sine alterius adminiculo se valeant sustentare."

performed throughout all succeeding ages. The main question was,—under whose superintendence and direction these objects could be most securely carried out and perpetuated? This question appears to have been fully thought over, and not hastily decided. At length, in A.D. 1151, by an instrument in which he recites the previous confirmations of Innocent and Lucius, DE BLOIS solemnly delivers up the care of his newly constituted Hospital to the providence of God; and then grants the administration of it to the venerable in Christ the lord Raymund, Master of the Hospital of Jerusalem, and his brethren, in regular succession for ever. How far the good Bishop made a wise selection in the comptrollers and administrators of his charity, we may be enabled to determine better as we proceed. At least he acted for the best; and the Hospitallers of St. John were deemed to have the management of such institutions under their special care.

DE BLOIS lived for more than twenty years after this act; and no doubt personally superintended the construction, and the architectural details, of all the eastern portion and transepts of the magnificent church; as well as directed the charitable gifts which were there bestowed, dealing out his bread to the hungry, and clothing the naked with raiment. His eyes had now become dim by reason of age, after an active episcopate of forty-four years. But his liberality was not stinted; and we are told that he increased his charities to such an extent as scarcely to leave sufficient maintenance for himself and his servants.

———

"ONE charitable deed is father still
To many more:......and thus through time
The streams of wisdom and of charity
Are ever fed, still widening as they flow;
E'en as yon Itchen, whose translucent wave
In narrow bed these venerable walls
Now sweetly laves; then, widening through the vale
Far down a broad and ample water rolls
Into the friendly Solent. May DE BLOIS
Be cherished here till Itchen cease to flow!"

ADMINISTRATION BY THE KNIGHTS HOSPITALLERS OF ST. JOHN OF JERUSALEM.

THE connection of St. Cross Hospital with the Brethren of St. John, commenced as already stated, was maintained more or less during the next century and a half, and was not finally renounced till A.D. 1303. Adrian IV (Pope from A.D. 1154 to 1159) formally assented to this arrangement, and confirmed the guardianship of the Hospital to Raymund of Jerusalem and his brethren. Pope Alexander III, the immediate successor of Adrian, followed, "after the steps of his predecessors of happy memory, Innocent, Lucius, Eugene, and Adrian," in his approval of the Hospital of the venerable Bishop of Winchester, who was then still living; and confirmed the custody of St. Cross to Walter, Prior of the Hospital of Jerusalem in England, and to his brethren.

In A.D. 1173, RICHARD TOCLIVE succeeded DE BLOIS. The new Bishop was quite alive to the welfare of his predecessor's work at St. Cross; but he was not content with its management by the Hospitallers. And, after some disputes, an agreement was entered into between the Bishop and the Knights Hospitallers, on the intervention of King Henry II, in A.D. 1185. The good Bishop on his part added one hundred poor persons to the hundred and thirteen already provided for: he assigned for the sustentation of the Hospital of Jerusalem, and of the poor of Christ in that Hospital perpetually, the rent of fifty silver marks; and absolved the brethren of St. John for ever from the payment of the yearly pension of ten marks of silver, and of two large altar candles of ten pounds of wax, which they were accustomed to pay yearly to the monks of St. Swithin for the House of St. Cross: while, on the other hand, the Knights entirely resigned their claims to the Hospital and its administration into the hands of the Bishop, never at any future time to demand the same of him or his successors. "Now this transaction "took place in the year of the incarnation of our Lord, one thousand one hundred "and eighty-five, the fourth before the Ides of April, in the pontificate of Pope "Lucius III, in the thirty-first year of the reign of Henry the Second, King of "England, at Dover; Heraclius, the Patriarch of Jerusalem, and Roger de Molins,

"Master of the Brethren of Jerusalem, then in England, being there present:—these
"being witnesses; Henry, the illustrious King of England, Heraclius, the Patriarch
"of Jerusalem, John, Bishop of Norwich, Randulf de Granville, Justiciary of the
"Lord the King in England, Herbert, Archdeacon of Canterbury, etc."

Only two years afterwards, Clement III, just raised to the papal chair,
completely upset this arrangement, and restored the administration of St. Cross to
Canerius, Prior of the Hospital of Jerusalem in England, with the addition of
sundry privileges : as, for example ; "When there is a general interdict in the land,
"having closed the doors, and shut out the excommunicate and interdicted, you may
"then celebrate Divine Service with a suppressed voice, and no bells sounding. You
"may also receive clerks or laymen fleeing from the secular power, freely and
"absolutely ; and retain them in your college without contradiction from any one."

On the accession of Richard to his father's throne, in A.D. 1189, he confirmed
by royal charter " to God, and St. John the Baptist, and the Brethren of the Hospital
"of Jerusalem, the House of the Holy Cross near Winchester, with all its
"appurtenances,—in churches and lands, in wood and plain, in meadows and
"pastures, in waters and mills, in ways and paths, and in all other places, and in all
"other things, with all their liberties and free customs,"—in the presence of the
Archbishop of Canterbury, and numerous Bishops and Earls, and David, brother
of the King of Scotland.

A few years later than this, in the pontificate of Celestine III, (A.D. 1197,) in
consequence of a complete misunderstanding between Godfrey de Lucy, the next
Bishop of Winchester, and the Hospitallers of St. John, a commission was issued
by the Pope to the Bishops of London and Lincoln, and Hugh, Abbot of Reading,
to investigate carefully the whole case in dispute; the respective parties, on the
appointment of Gilbert de Vere as Prior, appearing in the presence of the said
commissioners "at Windsor, on the morrow of the Sunday in which *Cantate
Domino* * is sung." It was then proposed by the commission that the Hospitallers
of St. John should, for certain compensation, (thirty pounds annually towards the
support of the poor at Jerusalem, or for home purposes,) utterly renounce the rights
they claimed in the custody and administration of St. Cross. Before acceding to
such a proposal they asked time to gain the consent of their Preceptor, Garcia de

---

* Readers of mediæval chronicles will observe that many Sundays are distinguished solely by the names
of the anthems or introits sung on them; thus:—(from Roger de Hoveden)—"on the Lord's Day before
'Lætare Jerusalem' is sung." Sundays were called, "Dominica jubilate," "Dominica resurrexi," "Dominica
cantate," and so on. See Noake's Monastery and Cathedral of Worcester, page 268.

Lycia, then abroad. After repeated delays from one festival to another, and one or two curious, if not amusing incidents,† the Commissioners "by the advice of men prudent and learned in the law," proceeded to pass judgment against the aforesaid Prior and Brethren, and relieved the Bishop of Winchester from all interference on their part touching the said House of Holy Cross; saving in all other things the constitutions of Henry, formerly Bishop of Winchester, of good memory, concerning the exhibition of the poor and their support.

Henceforth the control of the Knights practically ceased. And soon afterwards we find the succeeding Bishop of Winchester, Peter de Rupibus (A.D. 1204), acting with complete independence, and appointing his own Master, ALAN DE STOKE, the first whose appointment is distinctly chronicled. The terms of the appointment will be interesting in extenso :—

"To all the faithful in Christ, Peter, by the grace of God, Bishop of Winchester,
"eternal greeting in the Lord. Among the works of piety it is not esteemed the
"least when the benefit of the poor is respected, and their support so provided for
"that it may with prudent discernment continue and remain; the Scripture bearing
"witness, which declares, 'Blessed is the man who considereth the poor and needy,
"the Lord shall deliver him in the time of trouble.' Wherefore we, desirous to
"take heed that the distribution of alms to be made to the Poor of Christ by the
"constitution of the Lord Henry the Bishop, in the House of St. Cross, Winchester,
"may not be defrauded or perish, have elected Mr. Alan de Stoke, whom we know
"to be a prudent and faithful man, and have committed to him the cure of the
"said House with the appurtenances, to have and to hold freely, and quietly, and
"peaceably for the whole time of his life, saving to us and to our successors our
"authority and dignity therein. And, in testimony of this appointment, we have
"made to him the present charter confirmed with our seal."

It was towards the close of this (thirteenth) century that the western portions of the church were brought to something like a state of completion, and the magnificent west window added, during the Mastership of PETER DE SANCTA MARIA ; whose decorated tomb, with its handsome canopy once highly enriched with colour, forms a conspicuous feature in the north aisle of the nave. The purbeck marble coffin is still there : and within the recollection of a lady yet alive the body

† "They had sent, as they said, two of their brethren to the aforesaid Preceptor ; one of whom stayed behind in parts beyond the sea, and the other, being returned, fell into such sickness that he was not in his senses, and therefore they could not be certified by him."

of the venerable occupant was found entire, and even the features perfect. The body itself did not endure exposure, but shreds of the costly cope were long preserved. The purbeck cover, which had been unfortunately broken, has been replaced in stone, with the name and date A.D. 1295. The old inscription was, " Hic jacet magister PETRUS DE SANCTA MARIA quondam custos hujus domus."

Thus the church, which had been "sumptuously begun" a hundred and fifty years before, was at last brought to its present dimensions, and finished in the outline, and made completely available for Divine Worship throughout, though still, as we shall see, unfinished.

At the commencement of the next century, in A.D. 1303, the Knights Hospitallers, through "WILLIAM DE TOCHDALE, the humble Prior of the Hospital of St. John of Jerusalem," formally and finally relinquished all claim to St. Cross, in favour of JOHN DE PONTISSARA, Bishop of Winchester, by an Instrument dated "the second nones of June, in the 31st year of the reign of King Edward the son of King Henry."

✤✤✤

THE EARLY DIFFICULTIES.

ALL obstacles in the way of the progress and prosperity of St. Cross were not, however, removed by the completion of the church or the final expulsion of the Knights. ROBERT DE MAYDENESTAN was now Master; and, from an enquiry made by Bishop Henry Woodcock in the first year of his consecration (A.D. 1304), it would appear that considerable abuses had already crept in. Sentence of deprivation was subsequently pronounced against Maydenestan; and a few days later the Bishop issued a mandate for the admission of Gilbert le Forester, Mr. John de Fareham, and Robert de Colynch priest, as brethren of the said House.

It was just at this period that Pope Clement V (A.D. 1305—1316) issued his Constitution, "Quia contingit," * to remedy the misappropriation, waste, and negligence, which was evidently becoming general in the management of "Houses for the reception of strangers, Leper-houses, Alms-houses, or Hospitals;" and ordering "Inventories of the goods of such places, and a yearly account of the administration, to be rendered to the Ordinaries."

In A.D. 1321, Bishop Reginald de Asserio caused an enquiry to be made concerning the defects of the House at St. Cross, and for what it might be duly repaired. At this time GEOFFREY DE WELLEFORD was instituted on the presentation of King Edward II, on the plea that the See of Winchester was vacant. It was not, however, without considerable opposition that he was admitted to the Mastership. Dying soon afterwards, he was succeeded by BERTRAND DE ASSERIO in the following year. Bertrand was followed by PETER DE GALICIANO; against whom, as "without canonical title and notoriously unfit for such custody," Bishop John de Stratford in the last year of his episcopacy took proceedings, after due citation, stating that the said "Master de Galiciano had misapplied the rents and profits of the House, in granting the same to suspected and foreign persons who take flight to foreign parts, to the known dilapidation of the goods of the said House, and subtraction of the alms." Consequently a sequestration of the goods and profits of the House of the Holy Cross was granted to Master Richard de Hyde, rector of the church of Wykeham, in October, A.D. 1333. Peter, however, gained the ear of the king, Edward III; and in A.D. 1335 a royal mandate was issued to the sergeant-at-arms to defend him, and collect his rents and profits, against all opposition.

---

* "Quia contingit"; so named from its Latin commencement. In English; "*Because it ofttimes happens that the Governors of Houses for the reception of strangers,*" etc.

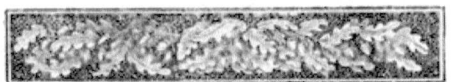

WILLIAM DE EDYNDON.

THIS great Master, afterwards Bishop of Winchester, succeeded Galliciano. Being at that time rector of Cheriton, an enquiry was issued by Bishop Adam de Orlton, in April A.D. 1336, to determine whether the custody of the Hospital was compatible with the Rectory : a question which the Commissioners, Alexander, Prior of the Church of Winton, and Master John de Uske, the official, decided in favour of the new Master ; on the ground that his custody had not the cure of souls annexed. After Edyndon had held possession of the Hospital for eight years and upwards, it was discovered by Pope Clement VI that, the previous Master having been a Chaplain of the Apostolic See, the appointment had canonically lapsed for that turn to the Pope. But, willing to shew the present occupant a special favour,—on account of his having " repaired the Hospital " buildings with costly work, and having expended many large sums of money in " that behalf, and in restoring to its former beauty " what he found decayed and ruinous,—Clement issued a commission, dated from Avignon, to induct Edyndon afresh, in due form.

An ancient register, still in possession of the Hospital, amply confirms the papal reference to the substantial work of Edyndon. He found the buildings, though sumptuous, in a collapsed and ruinous state ; and he set to work to repair them at great cost. He found the church still unfinished, and thatched with straw ; and he roofed the nave with lead : he also inserted the elegant clerestory windows, and glazed them ; and built anew two pinnacles at the west end. He built a chamber for the Master ; and roofed the " hundred mennes' hall." It was during his incumbency that William Byflete, rector of Morestead, gave a pulpit to the church. Byflete's pulpit has long since disappeared ; but is now not unworthily represented by a handsome structure of walnut and oak, designed by Mr. Butterfield, and presented by Mr. William Savage, of Winchester.

In the midst of his work, De Edyndon was raised to the episcopal throne of the diocese, which he filled with great credit. He was the first Prelate of the new Order of the Garter. He also commenced the rebuilding of the cathedral, which

c

was completed by Wykeham. He was succeeded at St. Cross by RAYMUND DE
PELEGRINI, a nominee of Pope Clement VI. The ceremony of induction is
minutely described, and may interest the reader. "On the 14th day of May, A.D.
"1345, after the hour of vespers, before the gate of the Hospital or House of St. Cross,
"near Winchester, in the presence of the notary public, and other witnesses, the
"venerable man Mr. Raymund Pelegrini, Canon of London, presented and exhibited
"certain letters apostolical;—to wit, one of grace, and another executory, of our
"lord the Pope, being true leaden bulls, sealed after the manner of the Roman
"Court, not vitiated nor cancelled, but free from all error and suspicion,—to the
"venerable man Mr. John de London, rector of the church of Esher in the diocese
"of Winchester, the sub-executor concerning the provision or grace in such process,
"together with other his colleagues." The Deed goes on to describe "the said
"letters apostolical; to wit, the one of grace with silken threads, and the other
"executory with canvass threads;"...and proceeds:—"Forthwith the said Mr. John,
"by the delivery of the principal door of the said Hospital, and afterwards of the
"bell-ropes, delivered into the hands of the said Mr. Raymund, did, by the
"apostolical authority committed to him, actually and effectually induct the said
"Mr. Raymund Pelegrini into the corporal possession of the same Hospital or
"House, and all its rights and appurtenances; and subsequently, the same Mr. John
"advancing to the high altar of the church, in fuller token of such possession,
"delivered and assigned to the said Mr. Raymund a book, to wit, a missal; and a
"chalice:......the rector of the church of Alresford, and others in very great
"numbers, the servants and ministers of the Hospital, being present."

"After these things, on the seventeenth day of the same month, at Southwark,
"at the manor of the reverend Father, the lord William, by the Grace of God,
"Bishop of Winchester,—in the presence of me, the notary public, and of the
"witnesses under-written, specially called for that purpose, to wit, Mr. John de
"Uske, rector of Burghclere, John de Beautre, rector of Freshwater, and John de
"London, rector of Esher, of the diocese of Winchester, — the aforesaid Mr.
"Raymund presented and exhibited the aforesaid letters and process to the said
"lord William, Bishop of Winchester, and requested that he would admit him as
"the true Master, or Warden, of the House of St. Cross. And the said Bishop,
"having reverently admitted the said letters, and diligently inspected them, did,
"as far as in him lay, admit the aforesaid Mr. Raymund, etc. These things were
"done, as above recited, in presence of the said witnesses. Upon all which matters
"the aforesaid Mr. Raymund requested me, the notary under-written, to make a
"public instrument. And I, Robert de Notyngham, clerk of the diocese of York,

"by apostolical authority public notary, was present at all and singular the "premises, together with the aforesaid witnesses."

How much one would like, by some magic charm, to recall that spectacle of more than five hundred years ago! The church itself looking much as it now does; its western pinnacles just completed, the nave-roof recently leaded, the fine west window in all its beauty. But how different all else! Beaufort's tower and refectory not built;—De Campeden's work not thought of;—the brethren's houses probably at the south and east sides of the church, where the marks of the original cloister, and the blocked up entrance to the south transept, still remain; and where the foundations of the old buildings may be traced. But let us look a little further. The external ceremony is over: the papal letters have been duly inspected, and are clearly "true leaden bulls, duly sealed, and free from error;" the silken and canvass threads are all right; the great western door is formally delivered. And now, the procession enters the church; and, after the bell has been tolled under the tower, how much we should like to follow Master John and Master Raymund in their advance to the high altar; and see the furniture and decorations and plate; and compare notes with the present aspect of things. But the vespers at St. Cross, and the quaint pomp and circumstance of five hundred years ago, are gone by for ever; and, however they may excite our imagination, can never be reproduced.

The Master, thus solemnly installed, was not long in office; for in the following February, RICHARD DE LUTESHULLE was presented by Bishop Edyndon, Raymund de Pelegrini having resigned his charge, by reason of exchange for the prebendal church of Gillingham, in the Diocese of Salisbury. He was succeeded, after three years, by JOHN DE EDYNDON, a nephew of the Bishop, in A.D. 1349.

WILLIAM OF WYKEHAM'S EPISCOPATE, AND JOHN DE CAMPEDEN'S RESTORATIONS.

THE distinguished Prelate, whose well-known statue heads this section, was a native of the Hampshire village that still retains the name which it conferred upon him, and which he has immortalised. After rendering essential services to King Edward III as an architect, especially in the improvement, or rather rebuilding, of Windsor castle, he was advanced to posts of higher importance; and at last, on the death of Edyndon, consecrated Bishop of Winchester, in A.D. 1366. He was also made Lord High Chancellor of England.

The name of this great man has been most widely disseminated in connection with the two noble Colleges, which he founded and endowed, at Winchester and Oxford. But he has also left the stamp of his character and energy on St. Cross. In the same year that he became Bishop the younger Edyndon was succeeded by WILLIAM DE STOWELLE, as Master of the Hospital. In the year following Stowelle effected an exchange with Sir RICHARD DE LYNTESFORD, rector of Burghclere. Not long afterwards Lyntesford proposed to make a further exchange with Sir

ROGER DE CLOUNE, rector of the church of Campsall, in the archdiocese of York : and William of Wykeham, being at that time "in many ways so occupied in various and difficult affairs of the king that he could not personally attend to the despatch of such exchange," duly commissioned the Archbishop, in his stead, to hear, examine, and fully discuss, the causes of the exchange; and to authorise it, if he approved. Whereupon De Cloune became Master, in A.D. 1370.

Two years later, when Wykeham had more leisure to examine personally into the affairs of St. Cross, he found that great irregularity and gross abuses had attended these repeated exchanges. He summoned Stowelle and Lyntesford successively before him, in the chapel of his manor of Highelere. And there, in the presence of John de Campeden, Canon of the church of Southwell, and many other discreet persons, they made their submission : and "swore, on the Holy Evangelists, "that they would in no wise contradict in right or fact the Bishop's decree, under "a penalty of £100 sterling; one moiety thereof to be applied to the exchequer "chamber of our lord the Pope, and the remaining moiety to the fabric of the "cathedral church of Winton," on the restoration of which the Bishop was so busily engaged. The following month the episcopal commissioners pronounced sentence against De Cloune, to the extent of deprivation; unless he should take the oath required by the Clementine constitution, (referred to in a previous section,) and make a faithful and full inventory of all the Hospital goods, and render an annual account of the profits to the Diocesan or his deputy. This sentence was resisted; and an appeal was made to the Pope, Gregory XI; who commissioned the Bishop of London to summon both parties before him, and settle the dispute. The Bishop constituted Dr. Thomas de Baketon, canon of Lincoln, his delegate; who affirmed the judgment of the previous court, and condemned De Cloune in the lawful expenses incurred. It is stated, in this judgment, that "four priests and "thirteen secular clerks have been used, and ought of ancient custom, to be "supported, to perform and minister there in divine offices; also one hundred poor "men; and the other goods of the same Hospital ought to be charitably distributed "to certain needy persons; saving the portion of the Master thereof, according to "the ancient foundation."

On the failure of De Cloune to establish his case he went abroad; and the Bishop managed the affairs of the Hospital by his kinsman and agent, NICHOLAS DE WYKEHAM, some nine years or more; until, on the death of the Ex-Master, he appointed his confidential friend and archdeacon, John de Campeden.

By the appointment of this excellent and energetic Master, the illustrious Bishop completed his good work for the Hospital; and earned the gratitude of all who, in succeeding ages, have been interested in St. Cross. The vigour and perseverance with which he recovered and restored to their original charitable purposes the revenues and possessions of this noble foundation, are but a small specimen of that devotion to business, and to all works of piety, education, liberality, and art, which has enshrined the name of Wykeham in the hearts, not of Wykehamists alone, but of all who have any connection with Winchester.

> "STILL to thy gentle spirit do belong
> The spots where thou didst live thy earthly span:
> And he who, musing, roams these haunts among
> Will still meet thee; and read, if read he can,
> The lesson of thy life,—that 'MANNERS MAKYTH MAN.'"

On the 4th of March, A.D. 1383, JOHN DE CAMPEDEN, Rector of Cheriton, in the person of his procurator, William, was inducted into the custody of the Hospital, by Sir Henry de Derneford, Steward of the Alms House or Hospital of the Holy Cross; on special condition of his making the required inventory, rendering the annual account, and duly administering the goods of the charity. The Bishop would have no further misunderstanding on this point: his directions are most explicit. "Our faithful son, Master John de Campeden, Bachelor in decrees, "rector of the parish church of Cheriton, in our diocese, is admitted by us to the "custody of the Hospital aforesaid; according to the form of the Clementine "constitution, 'Quia contingit,'......to make a faithful inventory of the goods of "the same House, and duly to administer the same goods, and also annually to "render a reasonable and true account thereof, according to the requirements of "the constitution aforesaid: and he has sworn so to do." On this occasion, "Sir "Henry, the steward, led William, the procurator, to the outer gate of the Close

"of the Hospital: and, by the delivery of the ring of the same gate, inducted him
"into the corporal possession of the said Alms House or Hospital, with all its
"rights and appurtenances; and committed to him the care and administration of
"all its spiritual and temporal goods. Then, leading him to the door of the
"church, he also gave and delivered the ring of such door: then, he delivered into
"his hands the cords of the bells; and the same procurator rang the said bells for
"a certain time. And immediately afterwards, leading him to the high altar, he
"gave and delivered up, as before, into the hands of the same procurator, the cups,
"books, vestments, and other ornaments of the church of the same Hospital; and
"assigned him a stall in the choir. Then the aforesaid Steward led him to the
"hall, to the place of the greatest honour, where the Master and chief Wardens of
"the same Hospital were used to sit at table at dinner time; and caused the same
"procurator to sit down; and made and monished the brethren, clerks, and other
"servants and ministers of the same House, humbly to obey, and deferentially to
"wait on, and serve with effect, the same procurator, as to the chief warden there."

In April, A.D. 1401, a careful inquisition was made into the extent and value
of the closes, gardens, and adjacent lands, belonging to the Hospital, and bounded
by what is termed, in that document, "the great river running towards Twyford,
"and so into the sea, commonly called Ichen-streeme." It mentions "the water
"mills of the same Hospital, called St. Cross mills;" and "the orchard, called the
"north garden, containing in length and breadth three acres and a half of land, and
"worth yearly three shillings and sixpence." Also "another garden, commonly
"called the porter's garden, containing twelve perches and a half of land; and
"worth yearly fourpence."

De Campeden was, like his patron Wykeham, an energetic builder; and soon
turned his attention both to the church, and to the hospital buildings generally.

In the seventh and eighth years of King Richard II, (A.D. 1384,) he built anew
the tower of the church; and roofed the chancel and the aisles. He constructed
the eight glazed windows in the lantern, beneath the belfry; and the sixteen lights
in the triforia of the choir. He entirely remodelled the interior arrangements of
the church; he erected fresh stalls, and a high altar of alabaster with a painted
reredos. He also paved* the church throughout; and fitted up one of the
chapels, with desks and forms, for the thirteen brethren. In the church alone the

---

* This gives the date (A.D. 1390) of the much admired and numerous encaustic tiles. Remnants of the
same patterns are to be seen in his church at Cheriton.

works were continued for five or six years. And indeed we may fairly say that the sacred edifice was brought to its *completion* by him, about 265 years after its foundation had been laid by De Blois. A very exact account of Campeden's work has been preserved in his register, and of the cost at which it was effected; very little short (it has been estimated) of £27,000 of our present money! An enormous sum under the circumstances of the case. For he tells us that during his incumbency the income of the Hospital was inadequate to meet its ordinary burdens.

De Campeden outlived his great patron by about five years, and died in the earlier portion of Beaufort's episcopate. He lies buried in the church which he so much loved, and so carefully adorned; and a magnificent monumental brass, in excellent preservation, perpetuates his memory; and has probably made his name familiar to many who have been little aware of his princely munificence.

The simple words which he has chosen for his monumental inscription, after his name and designation, are ;—

"I know that my Redeemer liveth, etc."—Job xix. 25, 27.

"Jesu, when Thou comest in judgment, condemn me not ;
Thou who fashionedst me, have mercy on me."

On his memorial slab, and elsewhere, in the place of armorial bearings he appears to have chosen the emblems of our Lord's passion, as shewn in the fourth and lowest shield beneath. The uppermost belongs to the first Founder De Blois. The other three, representing Wykeham, Campeden, and Beaufort, are found in the bosses of the nave vaulting.

CARDINAL BEAUFORT'S ENDOWMENTS AND NEW FOUNDATION.

—"In every household called The Cardinal!
Rich was his robe, his hat of flaming red;
And taller than the rest he seemed a head,
No Levite hard, nor bitter priest was he,
But from his cruse the oil and wine poured free:
And, when a mendicant in tattered weed
Knelt on his pavement in the hour of need,
His Almoner he called, with tender air,
And bade him make the suppliant his care."

CARDINAL BEAUFORT, at the recommendation of his half-brother, King Henry IV, was elevated to the See of Winchester, upon the death of the venerable Wykeham, in A.D. 1404. During all the earlier portion of the forty-three years that he held the See he was engrossed in other and less charitable works, which have gained him the reputation of an ambitious and unscrupulous statesman. But the care which the famous Cardinal bestowed, and the sacrifices he made in the latter years of his episcopate, upon the enlargement of St. Cross, and the munificent Foundation of Noble Poverty, form a redeeming feature in his character, even in the estimation of such as are least favourable to his memory.

For the endowment of his pious and cherished design, the ALMS HOUSE OF NOBLE POVERTY, he obtained a charter from his Nephew, King Henry VI: who, "on the second day of March, in the twenty-first year of his reign, gave licence to his "dear uncle, the venerable Father in Christ, Henry, Cardinal of England and Bishop "of Winchester, to grant and assign to the Master or Warden of the Hospital of the "Holy Cross, near Winchester, manors, lordships, and advowsons of churches, to "the value of *five hundred pounds yearly*, (a very large sum in those days,) in aid for

D

"ever of certain charges and works of piety there, according to the ordinances and "statutes of his said great uncle Henry, Cardinal of England." Beaufort, on his part, paid into the king's treasury 13,350 marks, as stated in the royal charter. The advowsons of the church of Crondall and St. Faith were shortly added to the endowment.

The formal Constitution of Beaufort's celebrated Alms House bears date February 4, A.D. 1446; to which considerable addition in the way of endowment was made on the 26th October of the same year. The following extract from the second document, bearing the later date, will give a sufficient idea of the Cardinal's noble design.

" Whereas, with the licence of the most christian prince, our lord King Henry VI, "and with the consent and assent of our beloved sons, Master THOMAS FOREST, "Bachelor of Laws, Master or Guardian of our Hospital of the Holy Cross, near "Winchester, and the Brethren of our said Hospital, we have founded within the "precincts thereof our certain Alms House, called of NOBLE POVERTY, of two "priests, thirty-five brethren, and three sisters, under the rule of the said Master "Thomas Forest, and his successors,—we have also charged to be observed, "fulfilled, and performed, certain devotions and observances expressed in our said "statutes." And then,—fearing that he had not done enough, and that the value of his gifts might, in tract of time, be diminished, and that so "irreparable ruin (which God forbid) might overtake the aforesaid House of Alms,"—he adds :— "So far, therefore, as with God's assistance we are able, wishing to provide against "such events of future loss and uncertain chances, we do grant, unite, annex, and "incorporate the parish church of Crondall, at present void by the death of "Master John Foxholds, the last rector thereof; also, the said Master of our said "Hospital we have inducted into the real and corporal possession of the said "church of Crondall, with its rights, with the consent of our archdeacon, by "delivery of our coif. And we, and our successors, Bishops of Winchester, will at "all future times for ever defend the induction of the said Master and his "successors." Then follows the annexation of the church of St. Faith, the Hospital of St. John, Fordingbridge, and the chapelries of Etchenswell, Cold Henley, and St. James's, Winchester.

Beaufort's buildings were quite commensurate with his other grandly conceived plans for the formation and perpetuation of his *Domus Eleemosynaria Nobilis Paupertatis.* The lofty and elegant gate-tower, which still bears his name; the finely proportioned refectory, with its imposing entrance; and the master's and brethren's houses, with their quaint chimneys. These are all noble specimens of his architecture; and justly entitle the royal Cardinal to take rank with his royal predecessor De Blois, as more than a benefactor, even a second Founder of St. Cross.

But, amid his benevolent schemes, his end was fast approaching; and death carried him off* without permitting him to witness their completion. The substantial buildings remain. But, alas! despite every precaution which he had taken, his noble design has never been really carried out to this day. The intentions of the donor, however, are not forgotten by those who are indebted to him for the place in which they dwell; and there is reason to hope that his last wishes may even yet be realised to a very considerable extent. What are termed his candlesticks and salt cellars are still preserved, with some old leathern jacks for beer, and are to be seen in the refectory. The chair attributed to him seems of later date.

---

* Shakspeare has done justice only to the darker features in the renowned Cardinal's portrait. We would take his sketch of the last scene in its most charitable interpretation.

> "*K. Henry.* PEACE to his soul, if God's good pleasure be!
> Lord Cardinal, if thou think'st on heaven's bliss,
> Hold up thy hand, make signal of thy hope!
> He dies, and makes no sign. O God, forgive him!
>
> *Warwick.* So bad a death argues a monstrous life.
>
> *K. Henry.* Forbear to judge, for we are sinners all."
>
> SECOND PART OF HENRY VI, *Act* iii.

An interesting inscription on brass, near the west entrance of the church, remains, to the memory of one of his faithful servants, as follows :—

"THE yere of oure Lord MCCCCL and two,
Upon the xi day, in the mouth of Feverer,
The soul of John Newles the body passed fro'.
A Brother of this place, restyng under yis stone here.
Born in beanie (?), squyer and servant more yan xxx yere
Unto Harry Beauford, Busshop and Cardinal.
Whos soules God convey, and his moder dere,
Unto the blisse of Heven that is eternal. Amen."

Cardinal Beaufort was succeeded by WILLIAM OF WAYNFLETE, in A.D. 1447. We find the new Bishop in the third year of his episcopate appointing two Brothers on "the New Foundation of Noble Poverty," in the room* of others of the same foundation, who (in his own words) had "gone the way of all flesh;" and again two others, very few years later. But it is evident that the scheme of the late Cardinal had never been fully carried out. On the contrary, in a royal charter of the 33d Henry VI, dated August 6, A.D. 1455, it is stated that "no such Alms- "House, within the site of the said Hospital of St. Cross, is founded or established ; "but it is probable such pious and devout intention of our said uncle will be "frustrated and brought to naught :" to prevent which "we have given licence "to William (Waynflete), now Bishop of Winchester, to erect and establish a "certain other perpetual Hospital, to be for ever called the *Alms House of Noble* "*Poverty* of Henry, Cardinal and Bishop of Winchester, son of John, Duke of

---

* There are still purbeck slabs within the communion rails, in memory of two Brothers of the "New Foundation of Henry, Bishop of Winton and Cardinal of England." The inscriptions are in Latin, and perfectly legible.

"Lancaster, of noble memory." By virtue of this licence from the Crown, a grant from Bishop Waynflete, May 12, A.D. 1460, confirms to the "warden, chaplains, brethren, and sisters, of the new Foundation" all the original property made over by the King.

But, just when we might have hoped for the completion of Beaufort's munificent plan, there was a serious change in the government of the country. For the following year the white rose supplanted the red; the House of York became dominant in the person of Edward VI; and the disastrous consequences to the charity are summed up in the sadly reduced scheme of Waynflete, published in the last year of his episcopate, August, A.D. 1486. "Although our most venerable "brother Henry, of good memory, our predecessor, had erected, etc.—yet in time, "and by the craft of succeeding persons, the lordships, rents, tenements, and "possessions, are wholly taken from the said Hospital, and *occupied by the power* "*of noble persons.* Hence, it being incumbent on us to have regard to divine "meditation, divine worship, etc.,......as the intention of our predecessor cannot be "wholly perfected on account of the reasons in these premises, and, having regard to "how far the advantages of such fruits and ecclesiastical benefices yet remain,—We "appoint and ordain, by our ordinary power, that from henceforth there shall be "there two brethren in charge of the private prayers in the said new Alms House, "like unto the ancient brethren, though differently clad; and one perpetual "chaplain at the presentation of the Master."

This is confirmed by PETER COURTNEY, the succeeding Bishop, in A.D. 1487, with some further particulars as to their allowances.—"We appoint from henceforth "that the chaplain receive ten marks, and each of the brethren sixty-six shillings "and eightpence, by the hands of the Master, to be paid quarterly: and "moreover, we allow yearly to the said poor persons ten shillings for their washing "and shaving; and to the Master, for overlooking and rule of the said chaplain "and brethren, we allow one hundred shillings of lawful English money."

In A.D. 1489, RICHARD HARWARD, Doctor of Laws, Master of the Hospital of St. Cross, "over which he had for a long space of time presided, did freely "resign the same House, on condition that provision and chambers be assigned to "him and to three of his servants, by authority of the Bishop, or his commissary "having lawful and sufficient power." Harward lived nearly four years after his resignation; and lies buried in the church where he is commemorated by a small brass on the north side of the chancel. He was succeeded by Dr. JOHN LYCHEFELD, the immediate predecessor of ROBERT SHERBORNE.

THE BEGINNING OF THE SIXTEENTH CENTURY.—TIMES OF BISHOP FOX AND ROBERT SHERBORNE.

RICHARD FOX was translated to the See of Winchester in the beginning of this century, A.D. 1501. He had been of essential service to Henry VII in less prosperous days, before his accession to the throne; and had been made Bishop of Exeter soon after the victory of Bosworth field, when Courtney was translated to Winchester. During the earlier years of Bishop Fox's episcopate ROBERT SHERBORNE, a native of the county and a Wykehamist, presided over St Cross. While the Bishop and Prior Silkstead were pursuing their noble and magnificent plans for the repairs and decoration of the eastern part of the cathedral, and rivalling the work of Wykeham and Edyndon in the nave, Robert Sherborne at St. Cross was following in the steps of De Campeden and Beaufort, and completing what was still unfinished there. His favourite motto, "Dilexi sapientiam," with his initials "R. S.," is found both carved in stone and painted in glass in several parts of the buildings, and in the windows. The specimen given is from the fire-place of the porter's lodge, with the date A.D. 1503. It occurs in the same form in the room above the lodge, supposed to have been the infirmary; and again, carved round the singular pillar which supports the charming little oriel window in the centre of the ambulatory. Indeed we may fairly suppose all the eastern side of the quadrangle, from the porter's lodge to the church, including the picturesque octagonal turret staircase, with its admixture of brick, stone, and flint, and the oaken piers which support the covered communication with the church, to have been the work of Sherborne. Subsequent alterations at the latter end of the seventeenth century, account for the stone which bears the name of a later Master, Henry Compton.

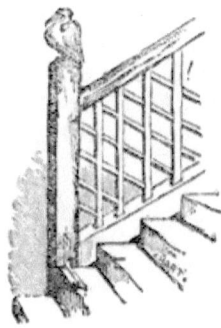

Annexed is an engraving of the hand-rail to the rough stone stairs which give access, at present, from the refectory to the Founder's chamber, or muniment room, over the gateway. And from the pelican, the well-known emblem of Bishop Fox, which surmounts the lower post, we may suppose this alteration in the stairs to be of the date of Fox and Sherborne. An alteration it evidently is, and of a ruder kind than the original work. In A.D. 1505 Sherborne was promoted to the bishopric of St. David's; and in A.D. 1508 to that of Chichester, where he spent large sums of money in beautifying his cathedral, and died in A.D. 1536.

At this time, in A.D. 1507, the parish church of St. Faith was pulled down, with the sanction of the Bishop. And it is said that the font and bell were removed to the Hospital-church, which has been in use among the parishioners ever since, as for all practical purposes their own church.

A monumental brass records that, in A.D. 1518, Thomas Lawne, Rector of Mottisfont, was buried in the church. But what connexion he had with the Hospital, or whether the priestly effigy, and the inscription beneath it, really belong to each other, is not at all evident.

JOHN CLAYMUND, a prebendary of Wells, of which cathedral Fox had been for a short time Bishop, was made Master of St. Cross, in A.D. 1517; and subsequently became the first President of Corpus Christi, the new College which Fox, following the example of some of his distinguished predecessors, had just erected in Oxford. This fact accounts for the memorandum in Wood, that the "Statutes of Corpus "Christi College, composed by the Founder, were publicly read before many "persons in the church of St. Cross, near Winchester."

On the resignation of Claymund, Master JOHN INCENT,* Vicar-general of the

---

* Or Innocent: made Dean of St. Paul's in 1537. His are a curious specimen of what Heralds denominate *speaking* Arms, viz.—"Argent on a bend gules, a fair and *innocent* virgin,......... with hair "loose about the shoulders, Or; her right hand holding two roses, and reaching over her head, and her left "extended before her person."

Diocese, was collated by Bishop Fox to the Mastership, on the 14th June, A.D. 1524. A few extracts from the carefully kept account of his Steward, William Pare, clerk, may prove interesting.   They date "from the Feast of St. Michael the Archangel, "in the seventeenth year of the reign of King Henry VIII, unto the same feast "next following in the eighteenth year of the same king, and in the third year "of Mr. John Incent."

	£	s	d
"Paid for bread, wine, and other necessaries for Divine Service within the Church this year...	4	19	5½
"To John Bridges for repairing the vestments and other ornaments of the said Church of St. Cross	0	12	9
"In money paid to John Rodford, Master of the Choristers, for divers necessaries by him bought and provided for the exhibition of the said Choristers..........	0	10	9
"And in money by the Steward in this year paid for divers other necessaries bought for the exhibition of the Choristers, as appears in the book of purchases	106		9½
"In a reward given to the parishioners of Twyford coming with banners at the Feast of Whitsuntide last past	0	0	12 "

TIMES SUCCEEDING THE REFORMATION.

A STIRRING period had now arrived. The revival of literature had a vast influence upon religion; and nowhere were the consequences more marked than in this country. Henry was no longer the champion of the Papacy. In this state of things, on the 20th of September, A.D. 1535, a Visitation of the Hospital was made by Dr. Thomas Leigh, "Commissary of the famous and honourable man, Master Thomas Cromwell, Visitor-General of the most illustrious Prince in Christ, Henry VIII. Such a visitation was no light matter to the religious houses of that day; and, for the most part, was the precursor of their dissolution. But St. Cross endured the scrutiny of the Visitor-General; who only found "certain things requiring reformation." After referring to the qualifications and support of the thirteen Brothers, he orders that the "Poor men shall have sufficient and proper "clothing and food within the said House, according to the will of the Founder, "and that it *be not given them in money* counted in any manner for the same. "Also, that the hundred-hall-poor shall not be served at the gates as mendicants, "like as was not long ago accustomed to be done; and such dinners shall be "distributed to them who study and labour with all their strength at handywork "to obtain food: and, in no case, shall such alms be afforded to strong, robust, "and indolent mendicants, like so many that wander about such places, who ought "rather to be driven away with staves, as drones and useless burdens upon the "earth. And also, some discreet and honest priest of the House shall hear and "teach the poor inhabitants here the Lord's prayer, and the Apostles' creed *in* "*English;* which prayer and creed all the poor men shall say together in the "Church before dinner. And also the Master, or President, shall not exhibit "reliques, images, or miracles, when sought for; but shall earnestly exhort pilgrims "and guests to give to the poor and needy what they would have offered for such "purposes. And also the Master shall in nowise diminish the number of the "priests, presbyters, sacrists, and others within this House, that have been used

E

"to minister here, on the Foundation, or by custom; and he shall observe all "and singular other things unbroken which the Foundation aforesaid, or laudable "custom, have hitherto required to be done here. Also, he shall have in this "House a library; in which, besides other necessary books, shall be placed "printed volumes of the New and Old Testaments, the works of Jerome, Augustine, "Theophylact, and others of the most ancient fathers of a similar kind." *

Yet, as a lingering vestige of departing Papistry, it is directed that, within the course of a month, a mass shall be said for the souls of the Founder, of the reigning King, and of Queen *Anne.* Poor Anne Boleyne, so soon to be hurried off the scene by the ruthless tyrant!

In regard to the temporal concerns of the Hospital, the Master was to deliver, before the ensuing Christmas, into the hands of the Vicar-General, the charters and muniments; together with an inventory of all its goods and effects, and a rental of its property. Such were the injunctions. Clearly Master Incent, and his steward William Pare, had their house and property in order: and no ill consequences accrued to St. Cross from that dreaded visitation of Thomas Cromwell and his Commissary: which, for so many ancient religious foundations, was the prelude of the coming storm which swept them clean away.

In A.D. 1545 WILLIAM MEDOWE, M.A., on the death of Incent, was appointed Master by Bishop Gardiner, in a form which begins thus;—"Stephen, by divine "permission, Bishop of Winchester, *fortified by the royal authority,* to our "beloved in Christ, William Medowe, etc." He was succeeded by Dr. JOHN LEFFE, in June, A.D. 1557; who, dying within two months, was followed by Dr. ROBERT RAYNOLDS, on the 24th August in the same year. After holding the custody of the Hospital but two years, (during which, however, he contrived to lease away a part of the corporate property, which it cost his successor in the trust much trouble to recover,) he was replaced by Dr. JOHN WATSON; who, after presiding at St. Cross for twenty-one years, was raised in his old age to the episcopal throne of the diocese.

Watson was of good service to the Hospital in procuring, after much pains and expense, a reversal of his predecessor's job in leasing away the Hospital property. It appears by an Act of Parliament of Elizabeth, (A.D. 1576,) that Raynolds "procured divers leases and estates unduly to be made, and sealed with the

---

* For some unexplained reason this not unimportant clause is partially erased in the original document.

"corporate seal of the Hospital, being in his custody, to one Ralph Cleverly, upon
"secret trust between them, absolutely for his own use:—not only of a great
"part of the Mansion House of the said Hospital, with the bakehouse and
"brewhouse, orchards, gardens, and closes adjoining, and heretofore kept in
"the proper occupation and use of the Hospital for the better housekeeping and
"sustentation of the poor; but also, of certain rents of wheat and malt, and also
"of one little manor called Ashton, of the yearly value of ten pounds." After
"divers great and troublesome suits in law, to the great travail and expense of
"John Watson, clerk, now Master of the said Hospital," it was enacted by
authority of Parliament, that both the said leases be made void, and of none effect
against the now Master and Brethren; and further, to avoid the like inconvenience
in time to come, at the humble request of the said John Watson, provision was
made to prevent the leasing out in future of the premises and lands within the
precincts of the Hospital of St. Cross and parish of St. Faith.

Master Watson appears to have made several members of his family serviceable
in the administration of the Hospital, as we gather from their names very neatly
carved upon one of the bookstands now in the south chapel of the choir.   First
there is the father, "John Watson, Master of this place"; next, "Sir John Watson,
Chanter;" then, "Sir Henrie Watson, Stewarde;" "Sir John Wrighte, Curate;"
and, finally, "R. Ganet, Singing-man; the year of Christ, 1572."   This proves,
by the way, that the choral service in the church of St. Cross survived the
Reformation, and had not fallen into desuetude in the reign of Queen Elizabeth.

The vacancy, caused by the elevation of Dr. Watson to the See of Winchester,
was filled by the appointment of ROBERT BENNETT; on whose becoming Bishop
of Hereford, in A.D. 1603, the Queen designated the Hon. George Brooke,
brother of Lord Cobham, as the future Master. But, Elizabeth dying, her successor,
James I, set aside the nomination in favour of one of his countrymen,
James Hudson; though eventually, in consequence of Hudson being a layman,
it was conferred upon ARTHUR LAKE, a brother of Sir Thomas Lake. Lake
became Bishop of Bath and Wells. And at length, in A.D. 1616, the King
succeeded in putting into St. Cross a countryman of his own, and, apparently, a
layman also, Sir PETER YOUNG, Knight. He had been Tutor to James; and, in
that capacity, had been placed about his person by friends of the episcopal church
to counteract the influence of his presbyterian Tutor, Buchanan. In a rough draft
of a lease of St. Cross, Sir Peter is described as one of His Majesty's Privy Council
in Scotland. His youngest son was made Dean of Winchester.

The oldest Register of births, marriages, and deaths now remaining to the Hospital begins with this curious notice of him, in the handwriting of John Hunt, the then Chaplain :—"The cause of the losse of the former Register, as far as I "can gather, was this :—When Sir Peter Young, a Scotchman, was Master of this "Hospital, which was in the dayes of King James, he, living in Scotland, left the "management of the concerns of this House to his sonne, Dr. Young, Dean of "Winton, who made one Mr. Wright both Chaplain and Steward. This Mr. Wright "dying, his widdow, whether out of fear of being brought to accounts, or out of "obedience to his commands is uncertain, burnt all his papers, and amongst them, "the Register also. Since which time to this there hath been no other bought. "Nor could this be had, though of so small a value, without a deal of struggling "and intreaty : so careless are the generality of men for public concerns, though "nearly respecting them and theirs.

"September 23, 1676.

"JOHN HUNT, Chaplain."

———

A fac-simile is presented below of the ancient Corporate Seal of the Hospital, mentioned in the thirty-eighth page. It is of silver. The arms of the Hospital are at the foot of the Cross. The legend round it may be translated ;—"The Seal of the Corporate House of the Holy Cross, near Winchester."

IN THE DAYS OF DR. LEWIS; AND DURING THE COMMONWEALTH.

IN A.D. 1627, the See of Winchester being void, Dr. WILLIAM LEWIS, Provost of Oriel from A.D. 1617 to 1621, was presented by King Charles I. to the Mastership "then vacant by the natural death of Peter Younge, Knight, the last possessor thereof." A few years after his appointment a stringent enquiry was made by Archbishop Laud, previous to "his Grace's Metropolitical Visitation in the Diocese of Winton." We feel sure no apology will be required for publishing, almost at full, these Articles of Enquiry, and "the Personall answere of the Master and others."

ARTICLES OF ENQUIRY.

1. Who is appointed by your Founder Visitor of your Hospital? Whether hath he power to punish such offences as are contrary to the Statutes, etc.

2. What are the yearly revenues of the said Hospital, with the wood-sales and all other extraordinary receipts?

3. What are the ordinary charges that go out thereof *singulis annis*, and what extraordinary?

ANSWERS.

1. To the first we answer that the Lord Bishop of Winton is appointed Visitor of our House, and hath all the power of a Visitor committed to him.

2. The yearly revenues and rents of the House amount to £200 per annum or thereabouts; and upon our leases are reserved besides for our provision, 100 quarters of wheat, and 120 quarters of malt, and a small tithe of the parish adjoining towards the keeping of our cattle. As for wood-sales and other extraordinary receipts, since this Master came to the place, which is now about 8 years, there have been none at all. So far from that, the Master to his great yearly charge hath been and is forced to buy at dear rates the fuel for brew-house, bakehouse, kitchen, hall, and his own expense; as also timber, which hath been used in great proportion, near 300 ton, for the repairs of the House: the only two woods that belong to the House having been by one of his predecessors leased out into 3 lives, and continued by the rest, which are still in being, for 6s. 8d. yearly rent; and almost all the timber trees, which were reserved, having been cut down by others, and used for fire, as some well remember.

3. The ordinary charge doth exceed the ordinary receipts of the House *singulis annis*, which the Master supplies out of his other means. For the extraordinary charge, it having been for the most part issued out in repairs of the Church and House, we refer to our answer to Article 15.

4. How many loads of wood are yearly felled, and to what uses converted?

5. How many beds are there for the Poor of the said Hospital; and what other goods, household stuff, and utensils?

6. Whether there be, belonging to the said Hospital, a common chest to keep all the dotations, charters, and evidences of the same Hospital?

7. Whether there be a perfect Terrier of lands and possessions?

8. What leases be there made of the same possessions; to whom and by whom, and when and for how many years, or on what other terms?

9. What fines have been taken for the said leases?

10. Whether any goods moveable or immoveable appertaining to the Hospital are sold away; and when, and by whom?

11. Whether have the Poor of the said Hospital their due allowance, according to the Ordinances and Statutes?

12. Have you taken any money for admittance of any of the Poor men?

Of what Officers, or Governors, and Almsfolks doth your Hospital consist?

13. Whether the Master, Officers, and Almsfolks have offended against the Statutes?

14. Have you Divine Service in your chapel or oratory on Sundays, Holidays, and other days, according to the Book of Common Prayer? How often have you sermons or lectures, etc.

4. Since this Master's coming, in seven years and upwards, there have been felled about 6 loads of small trees, when none other for that use could be bought, which have been employed in making a small part of the lath that hath been used in the new coverings of the whole House; and there are not many more left upon the grounds.

5. There are 13 beds for the Poor, for every one a bed, of those that are to be lodged within the House. What other goods, household stuff, and utensils there are appear in our *Inventory*, whereof the Register of the Bishop of Winchester keeps a duplicate.

6. There is a muniment house to keep all the dotations, charters, and evidences of our House, which have been formerly kept in some confusion, but are now disposed in better order.

7. A perfect Terrier of our lands and possessions we find none. But of that little temporal land which is now left, which yields about £10 a year rent, and is copyhold, we have given order for a perfect Terrier. The rest that belongs to us are tithes of appropriate churches.

8, 9. To the 8th and 9th we answer that there hath been no lease nor fine received yet in this Master's time. But all the leases that belong to the House, except one of the least, of about £10 per annum, have been by the three last Masters converted into, and continued in, the term of 3 lives. What fines have been taken by our predecessors, or how they have been employed, we know not. But there is little appearance that they have been employed upon the public; we found the House in such extreme ruin and dilapidation.

10. We know not of any.

11. The Poor of the Hospital have had, since this Master's time, their due and full allowance for meat, drink, lodgings, and apparel according to the Statutes; and much more from the Master's charity, upon divers occasions and accidents, or indisposition of any of them; and attendants and physician allowed them in their sickness, and diet at the Master's charge, which is not provided for by Statute.

12. We know that none hath been taken in our time for the places that have been chosen by this Master.

Our Hospital doth consist of a Master and 13 Brethren, a Chaplain and Steward; 12 out-Brethren, and 28 out-Sisters that are not lodged in the House; and 2 Probationers.

13. We know not of any thing wherein the Master hath offended. And if, at any time, any of the Officers or Almsfolks have offended, they have been punished by the Master.

14. We have Divine Service read in our chapel on Sundays and Holidays, and twice every week-day, according to the form of the Book of Common Prayer. Lectures we have none. Sermons we have at all the chief Festivals of the year, preached by the Master, and often at other times as his occasions permit. We have a Chaplain who, by our Statutes, is to perform Divine offices amongst us; which are also many times performed by the Master himself.

15. Is your Hospital, Chapel, and all other buildings belonging thereunto, kept in good repair? If not, by whose default is it?

15. The fabrick of our Church and House, both which are very large, and all outhouses (which were all found by this Master in great ruin and delapidation, towards which he received no allowance from his predecessor,) are now in far better repair than they have been within the memory of man. The chancel and two adjoining nisles of the church new rooft and leaded, and two aisles more adjoining to the body of the church likewise new rooft and covered: the windows of the church and chancel, which were for the most part stopt with board and mortar, new barred and glazed: and *organ* set up therein; the church, as also the cellar and other offices, newly paved; the four sides of the quadrangle stript and newly tiled; the brewhouse and bakehouse wholly stript and tiled, and newly repaired both with walls and timber; the barns and stables, and all the walls about the House now in covering, and the House beautified within and without, to the Master's great charge: wherein he hath expended out of his own purse, as appeareth by the Steward's accounts, about one thousand pounds, having had no extraordinary receipt by casualty, fine, or otherwise, towards his so extraordinary a charge; and yet much left to do about the Church and House.

16. Do any of you know anything concerning the said Hospital, or any part or member thereof, that is fit to be amended? Declare it, and free your consciences.

16. We know of nothing fit to be amended, in any part or member of the House, that is not caused so to be amended by the Master, or, in his absence, by the Steward.

Under ordinary circumstances a few more years would have probably re-imbursed Dr. Lewis for the great outlay which he was then making; and enlarged receipts would have enabled him to become a still larger benefactor to the House, over which he so worthily presided. But, even then the distant murmurings were faintly audible of a coming storm, which was to sweep over the whole land, and overturn, for the time, all existing authority in Church and State. Dr. Lewis, who was a Canon of the Cathedral, as well as Master of the Hospital, did not escape the consequences of the Great Rebellion; as the following extract from Milner shews. "Another of the Prebendaries was Dr. William Lewis, who had "been Provost of Oriel College. Nothing could have proved more untoward to "the views of our Winchester patriots had he conformed to the Covenant and "Directory. Happily, however, he proved an unshaken loyalist and churchman; "which furnished a pretext for dispossessing him of the rich Mastership of St. Cross: "a sinecure, which our Member of Parliament, John Lisle, Esq., thought he could "manage as well as any clergyman in the kingdom. He accordingly procured it "for himself, and enjoyed it until called up to the mock House of Lords, which "Cromwell had created; when the benefice was bestowed on John Cooke, the "Parliament's Solicitor-General, who drew up the indictment against the King at "his trial."

There are two quaintly inscribed monumental slabs of the Commonwealth period, in the south choir chapel, over the graves of the children of one Laurence. The inscriptions run :—

"SUSANA LAURENCE,
VAS CARNE VALENS.

A FLESH PREVAILING VESSEL FOUND
BEAUTIFIED TO LYE UNDER GROUND.

VIXIT, DEC. 13, 1647.
DEVIXIT, JAN. 18, 1650."

"GEORGIUS LAURENTIUS,
EGO UTI LAURUS RIGENS.

I UNDER LY AS LAUREL DRY.

VIXIT, OCT. 14, 1650.
DEVIXIT, SEPT. 29, 1651."

At the Restoration, Cooke lost his head as a regicide; and Dr. Lewis was reinstalled at St Cross. We could wish that he had left some memorandum of the condition in which he found the Hospital on his re-admission. In the absence of such evidence, we may suppose that he had, in many respects, to begin afresh his work of thirty years before. And what had become of his organ? Had he only to retune it, or was it gone altogether? Certainly no vestige of it has survived. During the Commonwealth, organs were considered "squeaking abominations;" and were generally demolished by an ordinance dated A.D. 1644. That he filled his place with becoming dignity, and maintained a generous hospitality, is evidenced by the Steward's account books, which are still preserved. He survived his restored honours several years; and at last died on the seventh of July, A.D. 1667, just forty years after his original appointment. His monumental slab in the centre of the chancel records, in an elegant Latin inscription, that, having experienced such marked changes of fortune, he bore them both with equal magnanimity.

AFTER THE RESTORATION OF THE MONARCHY.

THE first fresh Master after the Restoration was Dr. HENRY COMPTON, who succeeded Dr. Lewis, and was instituted by Bishop Morley on the 18th of November. Compton was a son of the brave Earl of Northampton, who, during the recent civil wars, had shed his blood for the royal cause. In A.D. 1674, Bishop Compton, who had been holding the Mastership with the See of Oxford, was promoted to that of London. He has left his name in more than one place upon the walls; and we may suppose, from the position of his initials, that he rebuilt the outer gateway and some adjacent buildings more useful than ornamental. As Bishop of London, he officiated, in the room of the Primate, Sancroft, at the coronation of William and Mary. He was one of the early patrons of the venerable Societies for Promoting Christian Knowledge, and the Propagation of the Gospel in foreign parts. The Burial Register records that "Mrs. Bridget Fowler, widdow, "housekeeper to the Right Rev. Father in God, Henry, Lord Bishop of London, "and Master of this House, dyed March 23, and was buried March 25, A.D 1676."

On the advancement of Compton to the See of London, Bishop Morley presented Dr. WILLIAM HARRISON, on the 22nd February, A.D. 1675; and re-admitted him in May the same year, on the presentation of the crown, which according to usage claimed the next turn under those circumstances. Harrison dying on the 7th of August, A.D. 1691, was followed by Dr. ABRAHAM MARKLAND; who occupied the Master's seat for the space of thirty-four years, at the close of the seventeenth and beginning of the eighteenth centuries. At the commencement of his incumbency, on the plea that no written statutes for the government and regulation of the Hospital could be found, the famous *Consuetudinarium*, or "Customary," was drawn up, upon the testimony of the brethren, and of one Mr. Complin, steward for the last 36 years, and then aged 72. In this document, the Officers and recipients of the charity are enumerated precisely as in Answer 12 of Dr. Lewis to Archbishop Laud's enquiry. The diet and allowances of the brethren are very minutely recorded, both for ordinary and extraordinary occasions. An extract in reference to the latter will be interesting;

F

the more so, as it describes, with few alterations, the present custom. "That
"there are five Festival days in the year, to wit,—All Saints, Christmas, New Year's-
"day, Twelfth-day, and Candlemas-day: on which days the brethren have extra-
"ordinary commons, and on the eve of which days they have a fire of charcoal in
"the Common Hall, and one jack of six quarts and one pint of beer extraordinary,
"to drink together by the fire. And on the said Feast-days they have a fire at
"dinner, and another at supper in the said hall; and they have a sirloin of beef
"roasted, weighing forty-six pounds and a half, and three large mince pies,* and
"plum broth, and three joints of mutton for their supper, and six quarts and one
"pint of beer extraordinary at dinner, and six quarts and one pint of beer after
"dinner, by the fireside; six quarts and a pint at supper, and the like after
"supper. And on Wednesdays before Shrove-Tuesdays at dinner every brother
"hath a pancake; and on Shrove-Tuesdays at dinner every brother hath a pancake
"besides his commons of beef, and six quarts and one pint of beer extraordinary,
"among them all; and at supper their mutton is roasted, and three hens roasted,
"and six quarts and a pint of beer extraordinary. And in Lent-time every
"brother hath in lieu of his commons eight shillings in money paid. And on
"Palm Sunday the brethren have a green fish, of the value of three shillings and
"fourpence, and their pot of milk pottage with three pounds of rice boiled in it,
"and three pies with twenty-four herrings baked in them, and six quarts and one
"pint of beer extraordinary. And they have on Good Friday, at dinner, in their
"pot of beer a cast of bread sliced, and three pounds of honey, boiled altogether,
"which they call honey sop.........And also every brother receives quarterly eight
"shillings;—viz, six shillings and eightpence for himself, and sixteenpence to pay
"his laundress; and four shillings paid among them yearly by the tenants of
"Yately. Also, there is allowed by the Master three shillings and fourpence
"quarterly to a barber, for the trimming of the brothers. And upon sealing and
"renewing of leases each brother is to have twopence in the pound, for so many
"pounds as the fine for renewing the lease amounts to. And at Christmas, yearly,
"every brother hath a new gown made of black cloth rash, of five shillings the yard."

Moreover, "That it hath been the custom and usage, and now is, that there
"should be a Steward of the said Hospital, who is appointed by the Master for the
"time being. And, upon his entrance into the stewardship, he is to take the oath
"of the House to be faithful and true to the Master and Brethren; and to receive

* "The ingredients of the mince pies and of the plum broth:—two legs of mutton, (12lb weight,) 6lb of
"beef suet, 3 gallons of fine flour, 3lb of butter, 3lb of currants, 3lb of sun raisins, 2lb of prunes, 1oz. of
"nutmeg, 1oz. of cinnamon, 1oz. of ginger, 1oz. of cloves, 1oz. of mace, 1lb of sugar."

"the rents, pensions, and all dues and profits belonging to the Hospital; and from
"time to time to pay the Chaplain, Brethren, Hundred Hall, and all others belonging
"to the said Hospital; and, upon demand, to give the Master a true account thereof.
"In the Master's absence he directs and governs all things and all persons in the
"said Hospital; and he hath power to punish any of the Brethren and Hundred
"Hall, for any misdemeanor, by sconsing them their commons. He ought to have
"a chamber in the said Hospital, with convenient furniture, fire and candle, by the
"Master's appointment; and he is to have his diet with the Master, and in his
"absence to diet with the Chaplain. He is to have a salary of eight pounds
"thirteen shillings and fourpence per annum, to be paid him quarterly."

It proceeds;—"That it hath been the custom and usage, and now is, that
"there should be a Chaplain in the said Hospital, to be appointed by the Master
"for the time being, who is to be in orders of the Church of England. His duty
"is to read prayers in the Church twice a day, to visit the sick in the parish adjoin-
"ing and in the Hospital, and to assist the Master on all necessary occasions. He
"is to have a chamber in the Hospital, with convenient furniture, fire and candle,
"by the Master's appointment; and to diet with the Master, but in his absence
"with the Steward. His salary is ten pounds a year, to be paid quarterly."

Thirty years later the arrangement with the Chaplain was somewhat varied,
as will be seen in the following entry from the Register, in A.D. 1725 :—

"The REV. MR. THOMAS WILLIAMS, A.B., Vicar of Lancing in the County of
"Sussex, succeeded Mr. Keble White, Chaplain of this Hospital, the 29th of
"September :—the said Mr. Williams being allowed twenty pounds per annum for
"his sallery, sixteen pounds for his dyett, with a corde of wood, and one hundred
"faggots, and his candles."

There is a provision that all the goods or personal estate of each deceased
Brother, whether in his possession at the time of death or not, become the property
of the Master for his own use. But the most important clause in this document,
and that which was most strongly animadverted upon by the Master of the Rolls
in his judgment, is that one which directs that, after the Master has provided for
the Brethren and other customary charges, and kept the Church and House in
sufficient repair, he is to retain to himself all the surplus profits and revenues.
The "Customary" was sealed and signed by Bishop Mew * on the tenth of July,

---

* With the important proviso,—" always intending that nothing herein contained shall be construed to
" derogate from the Statutes of the Founder, if any such shall appear."

A.D. 1696; and ordered to be read publicly in the Hall once a year, on the 3rd day of May, (the Invention of the Cross,) before the Master, Brethren, Steward, and Chaplain.

It would appear, from his monumental inscription, that DR. MARKLAND added considerably to the appearance of the place by improving the gardens, as well as to the substantial comfort of the brethren by increasing their stipends. He appears also to have been a frequent and eloquent preacher in the pulpit. But the last deed recorded of him in the Burial Register is worthy of remark. The entry is as follows :—

"The REV. ABRAHAM MARKLAND, D.D., dyed the 29th of July, and was buried "the 31st of the said month. He was Master of this Hospital upwards of 33 years, "Prebendary of Winton about 50 years, and Rector of Meonstoke 47 years. *This* "*Church was whitewashed by the said Master, and finished about three weeks* "*before he expired,* A.D. 1728."

In Dr. Markland's time, the Hospital is thus described in "A Journey through England," published in A.D. 1723 :—

"At St. Cross there is an Hospital for the relief of Distressed Travellers, by "giving them a Manchet of Bread and a Pot of Beer, whoever calls for it. Car-"dinal Beaufort endowed it with a maintenance for a Master and thirty decayed "gentlemen Brothers. But since the late civil wars under King Charles I their number "is reduced to Fourteen. They wear black gowns, and go to prayers twice a day. "This Institution, like most others of the kind in England, hath fallen off from "the first design; for there are seldom any gentlemen amongst them. The Brothers "are put in at the pleasure of the Master, who lives like an Abbot; hath a very "good apartment, with fine gardens, adorned with a canal and evergreens; with his "coach-house and stables; and his income is computed to be a good £600 a year. "Besides he is generally a Prebend of the Cathedral Church of Winchester."

Born in the days of Charles I, Dr. Markland was Master in the reigns of William and Mary, Queen Anne, and the first two Georges; and "after a life of "83 years, passed very evenly in the midst of stormy days, prepared for Heaven, "he fell asleep in Christ." He lies buried in the chancel, beside his distinguished predecessor, Dr. Lewis.

FROM THE EARLIER PORTION OF THE LAST CENTURY TO THE PRESENT TIME.

DR. JOHN LYNCH succeeded Markland, being the first of the four Masters appointed in the last century. He was instituted August 10, A.D. 1728, on the presentation of Archbishop Wake, who had selected St. Cross as his option. During his rule, in A.D. 1744, on the representation of the Master and Brethren "that the chapel of the Hospital is a very wet and damp place, and the brethren "thereof very ancient men unable to attend evening prayer without manifest hazard "and danger of their health and lives," the second service on week days was relaxed. But, in lieu thereof, a sermon was to be preached weekly, instead of "only "on every other Lord's day; the inhabitants of the parish of St. Faith, the village "of St. Cross, and the hundred of Sparkeford, being now more numerous than "when the previous customs were set forth, and having no other place to resort to "for public worship but the said chapel, which they are permitted to attend for "the performance of divine offices."

On the decease of Dr. Lynch, in A.D. 1760, the well-known Bishop Hoadly, (just before the close of his episcopate,) collated his relative, DR. JOHN HOADLY, then Chancellor of the Diocese. Early in Chancellor Hoadly's Mastership a Commission was issued to examine and report upon "the buildings between the "porter's lodge and the church, which had become burdensome and useless;" and licence was given by the Bishop "to pull down and destroy the said buildings, "converting the materials thereof to the use of the Hospital." Happily this licence was never acted upon. One of the most picturesque portions of the Hospital would have been lost by the demolition of the eastern side of the quadrangle.

Dr. Hoadly held this preferment till his death, in A.D. 1776, when DR. BEILBY PORTEUS was, on the 2nd May, "admitted and instituted, on the presentation of "the Archbishop of Canterbury and the Bishop of London, Patrons for that turn, "as trustees under the will of the late Archbishop Secker, for the disposal of his "options.* Dr. Porteus held St. Cross along with the bishopric of Chester; and

---

* It was the custom for every Archbishop of Canterbury, besides his own patronage, to make his option of one piece of preferment in the patronage of each of his suffragan Bishops, to which he claimed the next presentation when a vacancy occurred. That St. Cross should have been, on more than one occasion, the selected preferment out of the Winchester Diocese, is an evidence of the consideration in which it was held.

"in his episcopal character consecrated the comparatively modern piece of burial
"ground at the south-east angle of the church.   Bishop Porteus enjoyed the
"retirement of St. Cross; and is reputed to have planted some of the elms in the
"park.   There were those living when the present Master came, who could
"remember his sermons and lectures in the Church of the Hospital.   But in little
"more than ten years Bishop Porteus was translated to the more important See of
"London, which he so worthily filled till his death, in A.D. 1808."

On the 18th of March, A.D. 1788, Dr. JOHN LOCKMAN, one of the Canons of
Windsor, succeeded to the Mastership, then "void, by the translation of the Right
"Rev. Beilby Porteus, Lord Bishop of Chester to the See of London; the
"presentation for that turn lapsing to our Sovereign Lord, George the Third, etc."

The next year, under faculty from the Bishop, the south side of the quadrangle,
between the church and the brothers' rooms, which was uninhabited and had
become very ruinous, was removed, "in order to admit the sun into the courtyard,
and add to the dryness of the building."   There were those, not long since, who
remembered that portion of the buildings: amongst them, the late respected
Warden of New College, Dr. Williams.

It was in A.D. 1792 that Dr. Lockman, in consequence of a dispute with his
Chaplain, submitted the *Consuetudinarium*, and other documents relative to the
Hospital, for the legal opinion of an eminent ecclesiastical judge, Sir W. Wynne;
who advised him that the system of leasing out the Hospital property on lives
could not be justified, and recommended a petition to the court of chancery as to
the proper application of the funds, with the view of averting more serious
consequences resulting from delay.   Had the then Master taken this advice, he
might have anticipated, with advantage to the charity, the far more costly (and for
the time almost ruinous) suit which followed some sixty years later.

During the earlier part of Dr. Lockman's time, the Master's house was occupied
by the then Speaker of the House of Commons, Charles Wolfran Cornwall. He
lies buried with his wife in the centre of the nave.   A small square of white
marble marks the exact spot, and is engraved with the initials C.W.C. and E.C.
The larger mural monument, adorned with the arms and insignia of office, is in
the south aisle, and somewhat out of keeping with the rest of the church.   He
succeeded Sir F. Norton as Speaker in the Parliament of A.D. 1780, and was
re-elected in A.D. 1784.   He died in A.D. 1789, and was followed by Speakers
Grenville and Addington.   The Chaplain, Mr. Rawlins, records, in the burial entry,

that "he filled the Speaker's chair with uncommon dignity, and sat in it for the "last time but four days before his death. During the recess of Parliament, he "lived here in the Master's house, as his former residence of Barton Priors was too "small for his retinue, since his advancement to the chair. The Speaker, in his "person, was handsome, tall, and comely; and in his manners extremely affable, "polite, and engaging."

On the death of Dr. Lockman, in A.D. 1807, Bishop North conferred the place upon his son FRANCIS NORTH, who subsequently became the EARL OF GUILFORD. He continued the old system of renewing leases on lives; receiving large immediate fines, but temporarily alienating the property, and leaving the charity but comparatively small reserved rents for its regular annual income. Forty years and more passed on, during the greater part of which, the late esteemed Chaplain, the Rev. W. T. Williams, discharged all the spiritual duties of the Hospital. During his last illness, in A.D. 1850, Mr. Williams was assisted by a former pupil, the Rev. H. Holloway; who, finding the previously-mentioned letters of Sir W. Wynne and other papers relating to the Hospital, placed them in the hands of Mr. Maule, the Solicitor to the Treasury, who sent them to the late Lord Langdale. Three years afterwards the matter came on before the Master of the Rolls; and ended in the retirement of the noble and reverend occupant, as shewn by the following extract from the Act book of the diocese of Winchester:—"March 26th A.D. 1855. "The Bishop accepted the resignation made by the Right Honourable and Rev. "Francis, Earl of Guilford, Clerk, M.A., of the office of Master or Guardian of "the House or Hospital of St. Cross, near Winchester, in the County of "Southampton and diocese of Winchester, and declared the same void."

On the 16th of April, the present Master was formally collated by the Bishop, in presence of a notary public. On the 21st of the same month he was corporally inducted into the possession of the Church and House, by the Rev. William Menzies, Clerk, M.A., Rector of Winnal, in the presence of the brethren: and on the following day, Sunday, April 22nd, A.D. 1855, he read himself in, after the customary form; the late senior Brother, Peter Thomas Twynam Stubington, carrying the staff of office.

The form of collation is subjoined in full, as a supplement to that of Master Alan de Stoke, in A.D. 1204; given in the eighteenth page.

"Charles Richard, by divine permission Bishop of Winchester, to our beloved "in Christ, LEWIS MACNAUGHTAN HUMBERT, Clerk, M.A., greeting.—We do hereby "freely, and out of mere good will, confer on you the office of Master or Guardian

"of the House or Hospital of Saint Cross, near Winchester, in the County of
"Southampton and our diocese of Winchester, now vacant by the resignation of
"the Right Honourable and Rev. Francis, Earl of Guilford, Clerk, the last Master
"or Guardian thereof; and belonging to our donation or collation, in full right,
"by virtue of our Bishoprick.   And we admit you, the said Lewis Macnaughtan
"Humbert, Master or Guardian of the House or Hospital of Saint Cross aforesaid;
"and do rightly and canonically institute you in and to the same, and invest you
"with all its rights, members, and appurtenances: you having first duly sworn
"on the holy Evangelists to reject, refuse, and renounce, all and all manner of
"foreign jurisdiction, power, authority, and superiority; that you will be faithful,
"and bear true allegiance, to Her Majesty, Queen Victoria, according to the
"tenour and effect of an Act of Parliament made and published in that behalf;
"also, that you will pay true and canonical obedience to us and our successors,
"Bishops of Winchester, in all things lawful and honest; that you will duly and
"faithfully observe all the statutes, ordinances, and customs, of the said House or
"Hospital; and that you have not obtained the same by any simoniacal payment
"or contract whatsoever.   And we do, by these presents, commit unto you the
"cure, government, and administration, as well of the spirituals as temporals
"belonging to the said House or Hospital: saving always to ourselves our
"episcopal rights, and the dignity and honour of our Cathedral Church of
"Winchester.   In testimony whereof we have caused our Episcopal Seal to be
"hereunto affixed.   Dated this Sixteenth day of April, in the year of our Lord
"One Thousand Eight Hundred and Fifty-five, and of our Translation the
"twenty-eighth."

THE DOLES.

"SWEET streams of human charity will flow
For ages in their native purity.
Look at yon archway, which the hand of time
Has touched but to adorn:—the well-head there,
Which from King Stephen's brother, good De Blois,
Took rise, flows yet.—The houseless wanderer,
Foot-sore and famished, no sleek menial finds
To spurn him from that gate: the Brother there
Welcomes each outcast of the churlish world,
And for his hunger carves the wheaten loaf,
And fills the goblet to his thirsting lip;
Then speeds him on his way with friendly speech,
Kind words, whose every tone is charity:
And with a lighter heart and nimbler step
The poor man journeys on. The swallow knows
And cherishes the dome; for he fears not
Each spring to build his clayey tenement
Even in the hospitable porch,—Heaven wraps
These quiet walls in a sweet atmosphere
Of peace and love.
　　　　　Pass we beneath the lodge,
See where, with silver cross upon his breast,
The Porter stands."

THE stranger, entering by the large gates of the Hospital, passes the Porter's Lodge; and one of his first enquiries is for the dole of bread and beer, which has been there distributed to the wayfarer during so many centuries, and still is

G

given as in days of yore. The *daily* dole is thus spoken of, in a book already quoted, entitled "A Journey through England": — "At St. Cross there is a "Hospital for the relief of distressed travellers, by giving them a manchet of bread "and a pot of beer, whoever calls for it. The bread that is given to the travellers "is very good and white, as is the beer. They have fresh every day, and what is "left at night is given to the poor." At present, the *daily dole* at the Porter's lodge is two gallons of beer, and two loaves of bread, divided into thirty-two portions, supplying a horn of beer and a slice of bread to each wayfarer. This dole is given under the archway of Beaufort's tower, at the small doorway shewn in the illustration, at the visitor's left hand on entering. The Porter has the charge of the dole; and to him the traveller must now be introduced. Under the ancient system, one of the brethren always acted as porter : but by the new scheme it is provided that the Trustees shall appoint a regular porter to take charge of the buildings and premises, and be responsible for an amount of actual work beyond the strength and capacity of the aged brethren. The present Porter succeeded Mr. Prior, now of Chilcomb. He keeps the garden and premises in a very praiseworthy condition. In the summer months, he too frequently finds that the daily allowance barely suffices the wayfarers' demands; but in the winter, or at any other time, whatever remains at night is given to the poor in the immediate neighbourhood. The loaves are of the best wheaten bread; and the beer as good as can be brewed from three bushels of malt to the hogshead. Both are the same which are in daily use in the Hospital; each Brother, as well as the Cook and Porter, receiving a similar wheaten loaf and half-a-gallon of beer per diem.

The *extra doles* were six in number. They were distributed on All Saints'-eve, Christmas-eve, Easter-eve, Whitsun-eve, the Invention of the Cross, and the Founder's Obit, the 10th of August; on which occasions the outer gates were closed, and the applicants (sometimes eight hundred in number) admitted one by one at the smaller opening, thence called the dole gate. Each dole consisted of five bushels of flour, producing about four hundred loaves of twelve ounces each. The brethren received each two loaves for themselves, and one for each inmate of their dwellings; the Cook two loaves, the Brewer two loaves, the Barber seven loaves, the Steward and Chaplain six loaves each, the servers of the dole fourteen loaves each : and the remaining, about three hundred loaves, were distributed, one to each of the applicants, at the gate; any additional applicants receiving one half-penny each in lieu of the dole-bread. On these occasions all sorts of characters were mixed together. There were generally a number of chimney sweeps first, the crowd making way for them. But such gatherings were productive of considerable disorder; and they have been judiciously discontinued for the last ten years; the money saved being applied to the benefit of the "hundred-hall" poor: the reader of the earlier part of this book will be familiar with the name. There are twenty-five poor persons in the receipt of a shilling a week each from the Hospital. These are the existing representatives of the larger number who were formerly received daily at the hour of dinner. What is now the brewhouse, on the east side of the outer court, is supposed to have been formally the *Hundred-mennes Hall*, in which these numerous recipients of De Blois' bounty were in the olden time daily fed.

The daily dole at St. Cross is still distributed, not only to the ordinary applicant, but to pilgrims and travellers from all lands; none being more struck by it, as old Brother Stubington often remarked when he was porter, than American visitors, who always manifest a deep interest in our ancient Hospice. Even Royal wayfarers have not disdained to partake of its humble fare, as will be read with interest from the subjoined extract out of the Visitors' Book :—

"December 9th, 1857. *H.R.H. the Princess Royal* visited the Church and "Hospital, and partook of bread and beer." The Princess examined with much interest the ancient Triptych in the Hall: and was graciously pleased to receive from the Master a copy of a short Lecture, which he had then recently published, on the History and Antiquities of the Hospital.

"July 27th, 1861. *The Crown Prince and Princess of Prussia, with H.R.H.* "*the Princess Alice*, and party, visited the church, hall, and Master's house, and "partook of the customary dole." Their Royal Highnesses were graciously pleased to accept some copies of Mr. William Savage's "Guide to the Antiquities of Winchester," which had been prepared by him, in vellum and gold, in the hope of presenting them to Her Most Gracious Majesty herself, and to the late lamented Prince Consort; who, it had been rumoured on a previous occasion, were likely to honour the ancient city of Winchester with a visit.

"December 31st, 1862. *H.R.H. the Prince of Wales and Prince Louis of* "*Hesse*, attended by General Knollys and suite, visited the church, hall, and "Master's house, and partook of bread and beer." The Royal party, on this occasion, inspected the large collection of monumental brass-rubbings in the Master's gallery.

"August 21st, 1865. *H.M. Queen Emma* of the Sandwich Isles, attended by "her Chaplain and party, visited the church, hall, and Master's house, and "likewise received the dole."

NOTICES OF THE BROTHERS.

MILNER remarks in his history, that "the brethren of this venerable Institute, being happily destined to 'walk through the cool sequestered vale of life, have kept the noiseless tenor of their way' in succession, during almost eight centuries, without affording any materials for history." But, though their names are not emblazoned on the historic page, the story of the origin of St. Cross, and the narrative of its past fortunes, would be very incomplete without some notice of the venerable men, for whose maintenance and comfort it was first founded by De Blois, and afterwards extended by Beaufort.

We read of Gilbert le Forester, John de Farcham, and Robert de Colynch, among the brethren in A.D. 1304, appointed in a time of mismanagement by the fatherly care of Bishop Woodlock. Nearly a hundred and fifty years later than the appointments of Bishop Woodlock, we read of several brothers of "noble poverty" in Bishop Waynflete's episcopate, such as Henry Chambre, Richard Norreys, Richard Brian, Richard Vaughan, Richard Deryke (in the place of Jordan Browning expelled), Richard Sheldrake, John Grenewyche, Robert Barton, Thomas Lago, and William Thomas. These, with John Turke and John Knyght, whose monumental slabs are in the chancel, were are all members of the foundation of Noble Poverty. There was likewise the Cardinal's faithful servant John Newles, who died in A.D. 1452, a brother apparently of the old foundation. In the south transept is the memorial brass of "William Sandres, formerly Chaplain of the new "foundation of this College, who died 29 November, A.D. 1464." Also, of "Alexander "Ewart, late brother of this place, who departed this trancitorie lyfe to Allmighty "God the 17th daye of July, A.D. 1569."

At a later period "John Starkey, a Cheshire man, after thirty years' service "under foreign princes, and ten years in His Majesty's Guards, was chosen brother "of this Hospital, September, A.D. 1674." A century later, "January 20, A.D. 1771, "Robert Bartholomew, a brother of St. Cross Hospital, was buried. He was a "native of Sherborne, in Dorsetshire; had been a soldier in Queen Anne's reign; "and was at the taking of Gibraltar, in A.D. 1704. He was many years porter of "this Hospital, and died, aged ninety and upwards." An oil painting of Brother Bartholomew is to be seen in the porter's lodge, at the back of which his age is given as 102. Knights too, and aged clergymen, have found an asylum here;—as the following entries testify. "Sir Edward Richards, Knight, brother "of this Hospital, was buried January 27th, A.D. 1685," and "the Rev. Robert "Norwood, a brother of this Hospital, was buried, March 5th, A.D. 1727; he had "been *blind for several years.*" Of another brother, "William Coles, who had "officiated as clarke and porter, for the space of twelve years before his death," it is recorded that "he was an Alderman of Romsey, and had served the office of "Mayor of that town, where he had lived many years in great repute: but, meeting "with misfortunes, he met with a peaceful asylum within the walls of the "Hospital; where he ended his days at the age of seventy-two years." One further extract shall suffice. It relates to a somewhat eccentric brother, whose eccentricities were yet fresh in the remembrance of our former senior brother, Charles Matthews, who had seen what is described below when a lad:—

"November 28th, A.D. 1790. Richard Hart, brother of St. Cross Hospital, "was buried, aged eighty-one years. Brother Hart was a man of very singular "turn and disposition. He was interred in a coffin of cedar, made by himself twenty "years since, out of a plank of a Spanish man-of-war, which he purchased while a "carpenter at Portsmouth dockyard. He had written many texts of Scriptures "and religious verses on the outside. He kept it constantly in his room, drawn "up by pulleys to the ceiling over the window."

Interesting narratives and stirring incidents might be recorded of not a few who have worn the ancient silver cross and the black gown of this Hospital: for instance, of Brother JOHN WEBB, who has not long since passed away from us, at the advanced age of ninety-five years.* He had been present, as a ship's boy on board one of His Majesty's vessels, in the sea fight, which took place, April 12th, A.D. 1782, in the channel between the Islands of Martinique and Guadaloupe, when Admiral Rodney defeated the French fleet, then going to attack Jamaica, taking five ships of the line, and the Admiral, Count de Grasse.

Amongst the photographs are the portraits of four of the existing brothers; and they may be taken as a sample of the whole, and a very fair specimen of the kind of men who are gladly welcomed to share the benefits of this place, and who gratefully enjoy, in their declining years, its tranquil shade. Brother WILLIAM

---

* Instances of considerable longevity are by no means rare amongst the brethren. Richard Humber, (a namesake of the present Master minus the last letter of his name,) whose signature is attached to some alterations in the consuetudinarium made in June, A.D. 1782, reached the patriarchal age of ninety-eight, according to his tombstone; ninety-seven, by the Register. Since A.D. 1771, the St. Cross Register records fifteen burials of persons turned 90 years of age; ten men and five women.

PIPER was admitted under the late Master, sixteen years ago. He is now in his seventy-ninth year, and has filled the office of Sacristan since A.D. 1855. His father was a respectable yeoman farmer in the neighbourhood; and in Twyford churchyard, east of the great yew, the family gravestones, for generations, are to be found. He remembers well the good old days when, after primitive fashion, his father and mother walked at the head of their children and servants to church. Brother Piper has always taken the most lively interest in the church and parish. He and the senior brother alone remain of those appointed by Lord Guilford. He is devotedly attached to the present Master and his family, who have ever found him a faithful supporter and friend.

Brother JOHN GRIFFITHS was one of the first admitted under the present scheme, in A.D. 1857; and has been Exhibitor of the place since the retirement, from infirmity, of the late Brother Stubington. Of all the brotherhood he is probably the best known to visitors and strangers, from his official position. He is an admirable Cicerone; and, though he has reached the patriarchal age of eighty-six last birthday, few of our visitors would suppose, from his elastic step, his upright walk, and his ready memory, that he had reached fourscore. Having been for many years an artist and drawing-master in the Isle of Wight, he is peculiarly qualified for his place; and not unfrequently meets with former pupils and old friends. He is keenly alive to all that concerns his former profession, and takes the deepest interest in the annual catalogue of the Royal Academy. Since his admission, with somewhat failing powers of vision, he has executed two beautifully coloured drawings of the church for the Master, who greatly values his services, and rejoices in the measure of strength and energy which is still vouchsafed him; and who feels that, as an Exhibitor, Brother Griffiths will not easily be replaced.

Brother JAMES KING was elected in A.D. 1859. Having been a mason by trade, he has not only taken deep interest in the work of restoration, but has been of valuable service in carrying it forward. The cleansing of the north and south chapels of the choir, from the floor to the vaulting of the roof, was his own unaided work. For some months he was on scaffolding of his own contrivance, early and late, at his labour of love. And possibly, in the words of a correspondent of *The Hampshire Chronicle* at that time, it was "the sight of this venerable brother scraping away that moved the anonymous donor, 'Z. O,' to offer £500 towards the restoration of the choir;"—an offer which set the example that has been since so well followed by other friends. Brother King is now more than "four score;" and, although not quite so active as when he is supposed to have attracted the attention of "Z. O," some five years ago, is still eager for occupation; and, if not engaged in the church itself, may be found in his own rooms working up the old and displaced stone into emblematical ornaments and crosses. The Master knows his worth, and regards him as a fitting member of such a brotherhood; devoted to the church and place, always ready to give his full share of labour towards whatever object may be in hand; and, at the same time, in all that he does, simply seeking his divine Master's honour, and humbly waiting for His coming.

Brother J. F. WHITEBREAD, the last of the quartett, entered the fraternity at a considerably later period. After being twenty years librarian of the Hampshire Library at Portsmouth, he was most thankful, on the close of that Institution, with which he had been so long connected, to find an asylum at St. Cross. Not quite so advanced in years as the rest, and from the nature of his previous occupation, and from preference, having been more addicted to books, and literary pursuits, he has contributed his special share to the common stock, and proved a valuable addition to the little community. To the Master he has rendered effectual help, both by reading the lessons in church at the daily and Sunday services, and also by the use of his pen on many occasions. He may be well termed the "corresponding brother" of the Hospital; not merely writing to the Master in his absence, but, on a recent very interesting occasion, writing for him, when Her most gracious Majesty the Queen honoured the brethren by presenting to their library a handsome copy of her "Leaves from the Journal of our Life in the Highlands." Brother Whitebread is an efficient helper to our venerable and infirm librarian Brother MATON.

The present senior brother of the Hospital, WILLIAM TRIMBEE, is senior both by admission and by age, being now in his ninetieth year, and in the full possession of all his faculties; still capable of enjoying the calm retreat which Providence has granted him; and yet never forgetting that better Home beyond for which this should be a daily preparation.

———

"Sent come
To share the bounty of De Blois; and dwell
With the great spirits of the mighty dead,
Wykeham, De Campeden, Beaufort, and the rest,
Who, with the Founder, shared the pious work.
And the whole scene a beauteous calm pervades,
That woos the soul to pleasing serious thought;
While the church tower, with venerable grace,
Lifts from low cares the willing mind to heaven."

A LIST OF CONTEMPORARY BISHOPS OF WINCHESTER, AND MASTERS OF ST. CROSS.

A.D.	BISHOPS.	A.D.	MASTERS.	REMARKS.
1129	HENRY DE BLOIS			The custody of the Hospital remained, during this century, with the Master and Brethren of St. John of Jerusalem.
1173	RICHARD TOCLIVE			
1189	GODFREY DE LUCY			
1204	PETER DE RUPIBUS	120-	ALAN DE STOKE	Collated by Bishop Peter de Rupibus in the early part of his episcopate. The precise year unknown.
		——	HUMFREY DE MYLLERS	Collated by Bishop Peter de Rupibus.
		1241	HENRY DE SECUSIA	Appointed by King Henry III, the See being vacant.
1244	WILLIAM DE RALEIGH	——	GALFRID DE FERINGES	Collated by Bishop Raleigh, ante 1249. Vicar-General.
1250	ETHELMAR DE VALENCE	——	THOMAS DE COLCHESTER	Was Master A.D. 1260.
1262	JOHN DE GERVAISE			
1268	NICHOLAS DE ELY	——	STEPHEN DE WOTTON	Died A.D. 1275.
1282	JOHN DE PONTISSARA	1280	PETER DE SANCTO MARIO	Archdeacon of Surrey. Died A.D. 1296
		1296	WILLIAM DE WENLYNGE	Steward of the Bishop's house.
		1299	ROBERT DE MAYDENESTAN	Deprived A. D. 1305. Restored; and still Master A.D. 1313.
1305	HENRY WOODLOCK			
1316	JOHN DE SANDALE			
1320	RIGAUD DE ASSERIO	1321	GALFRID DE WELLEFORD	Presented by the King. Died A.D. 1322
		1322	BERTRAND DE ASSERIO	Collated, 31st August, A.D. 1322.
1323	JOHN DE STRATFORD	1332	PETER DE GALICIANO	Resigned A.D. 1334.
1333	ADAM DE ORLETON	1334	WILLIAM DE EDYNDON	Afterwards Bishop of Winchester.
1345	WILLIAM DE EDYNDON	1345	RAYMUND PELEGRINI	Exchanged with his successor.
		1346	RICHARD DE LUTESHALLE	
		1349	JOHN DE EDYNDON	Resigned A.D. 1366.
1367	WILLIAM DE WYKEHAM	1366	WILLIAM DE STOWELLE	Exchanged with his successor.
		1367	RICHARD DE LYNTESFORD	Exchanged with his successor.
		1370	ROGER DE CLOUNE	Deprived, December 5th, A.D. 1374.
		1374	NICHOLAS DE WYKEHAM	Managed the Hospital till de Cloune's death.
		1382	JOHN DE CAMPEDEN	Archdeacon of Surrey. Died A.D. 1410
1404	CARDINAL BEAUFORT	1410	JOHN FOREST	Afterwards Archdeacon of Surrey and Dean of Wells. Died A.D. 1440.
		——	THOMAS FOREST	Appointed in or before A.D. 1426. Died at St.Cross, in Nov. A.D. 1463.
1447	WILLIAM WAYNEFLETE	1463	THOMAS CHAUNDELER, S.T.P.	Resigned A. D. 1465. Warden of New College, Oxford
		1465	WILLIAM WESTBURY, S.T.B.	Provost of Eton College.
		——	RICHARD HARWARD, LL.D.	Ante 1474. Resigned A.D. 1489.
1486	PETER COURTENAY	1489	JOHN LYCHEFIELD, LL.D.	Resigned A.D. 1492.
1492	THOMAS LANGTON	1492	ROBERT SHERBORNE	Afterwards successively Bishop of St. David's, and of Chichester.

A.D.	BISHOPS.	A.D.	MASTERS.	REMARKS.
1501	RICHARD FOX	1508	JOHN CLAYMUND	First President of C.C.C., Oxford. Resigned A.D. 1524.
		1524	JOHN INCENT, LL.D.	Also Dean of St. Paul's. Died A.D. 1545
1529	CARDINAL WOLSEY			
1531	STEPHEN GARDINER	1545	WILLIAM MEDOWE, M.A.	Prebendary of Winchester Cathedral. Died A.D. 1557.
1551	JOHN POYNET		[stored.	
1553	STEPHEN GARDINER Re-			
1557	JOHN WHITE	1557	JOHN LEFFE, LL.D.	Died 19th August, A.D. 1557. Æt. 66.
		1557	ROBERT RAYNOLDS, LL.D.	Ejected on the accession of Queen Elizabeth.
		1559	JOHN WATSON, M.D.	Afterwards Bishop of Winchester, and held the Mastership by Royal Dispensation till A.D. 1583.
1561	ROBERT HORNE			
1580	JOHN WATSON	1583	ROBERT BENNETT, S.T.P.	Afterwards Bishop of Hereford.
1584	THOMAS COOPER			
1595	WILLIAM WICKHAM			
1596	WILLIAM DAY			
1597	THOMAS BILSON	1603	ARTHUR LAKE, S.T.B.	Afterwards Bishop of Bath and Wells.
1616	JAMES MONTAGUE	1616	SIR PETER YOUNGE, Knight	Installed 18th January, A.D. 1616-7.
1619	LANCELOT ANDREWES			
1627	RICHARD NEILE	1628	WILLIAM LEWIS, S.T.P. *	Dispossessed during the Commonwealth; but restored A.D. 1660; and died July 7th, A.D. 1660.
1632	WALTER CURLE			
1660	BRIAN DUPPA			
1662	GEORGE MORLEY	1660	HENRY COMPTON, D.D.	Afterwards successively Bishop of Oxford and of London.
		1676	WILLIAM HARRISON, D.D.	Prebendary of Winchester Cathedral. Died August 7th, A.D. 1694.
1684	PETER MEWS	1694	ABRAHAM MARKLAND, D.D.	Prebendary of Winchester Cathedral. Died July 29th, A.D. 1728.
1706	SIR J. TRELAWNEY			
1721	CHARLES TRIMNEL			
1723	RICHARD WILLIS	1728	JOHN LYNCH, D.D.	
1734	BENJAMIN HOADLY	1760	JOHN HOADLY, LL.D.	Chancellor of the Diocese, etc.
1761	JOHN THOMAS	1776	BEILBY PORTEUS, D.D.	Afterwards successively Bishop of Chester and of London.
1781	BROWNLOW NORTH	1788	JOHN LOCKMAN, D.D.	Canon of Windsor.
		1807	FRANCIS NORTH, M.A., Earl of Guilford	Resigned, March 20th, A.D. 1855.
1821	SIR GEORGE P. TOMLINE			
1827	CHARLES R. SUMNER	1855	LEWIS MACNAUGHTAN HUMBERT, M.A.	

A LIST OF THE RECTORS OF THE PARISH CHURCH OF ST. FAITH,

FROM THE TIME OF EDWARD I. TILL ITS INCORPORATION
WITH THE HOSPITAL OF ST. CROSS BY CARDINAL BEAUFORT, MARCH 6, A.D. 1446.

PATRONS.	A.D.	RECTORS.	REMARKS.
		JOHN BELLEGAMBE	Died, A.D. 1287.
JOHN DE PONTISSARA	1287	JOHN PAVON	
	———	HENRY DE LISKERED	Resigned, A.D. 1300.
	1300	HUGH DE LONDON	Resigned, A.D. 1320.
RIGAUD DE ASSERIO	1320	WILLIAM KNIGHT	Resigned, A.D. 1322.
	1322	ROBERT DE SANDALE	Died, A.D. 1342.
ADAM DE ORLETON	1342	RICHARD DE BYBURY	Resigned, A.D. 1342.
	1342	THOMAS DURLEYE	
WILLIAM DE EDYNDON	1349	NICHOLAS DE KYNGESTON	And Rector, A.D. 1357.
	1357	JOHN RACEBAS	
	1361	RICHARD LAURENCE	Died, A.D. 1381.
WILLIAM DE WYKEHAM	1381	WILLIAM DE ECHENESWELLE	
	1389	THOMAS LAVYNGTON	Resigned, A.D. 1389.
	1389	JOHN MASONN, *alias* SPISER	
	1390	THOMAS BUCKHURST	
	———	JOHN POMERY	Resigned, A.D. 1411.
CARDINAL BEAUFORT	1411	JOHN MOORE	

[For this list of Rectors, as well as for several important corrections and additions in the previous list of Masters, we are indebted to the kindness and researches of Francis Joseph Baigent Esq., of Winchester.]

PART II.

Present Aspect, and Existing Buildings.

"BELOVED St. Cross! where all the charms combine
That warm the canvass or that grace the line;
Thou kind retreat from sorrow and from care,
With sparkling waters and a balmy air;
Amid thy meadows green and peaceful shades,
Thy crowning hills and long deep bow'ry glades,
What troubled heart can fail in thee to find
Health for the body, solace to the mind."

IN the well watered valley of the Itchen, amid sunny hills and flowery meads, the position of St. Cross offers no exception to the proverbial sagacity with which our forefathers chose the sites of their religious houses and charitable foundations. Distant only a mile from the Cathedral City, and within a few yards of the high road to Southampton, the lofty Church of De Blois rises majestically from the midst of the domestic buildings, which are picturesquely grouped about it; and, fringed by luxuriant elms and magnificent walnut trees, presents an aspect as charming as it is imposing. Thus situated, it is a conspicuous object to the traveller approaching Winchester from various directions, and from a considerable distance. And on a nearer approach, the lower buildings, which cluster round the Church, add their full share to the general effect. This is more especially the case from the Southampton direction, whence the noble gateway of Beaufort, the refectory with its striking porch, and the long range of tall quaint chimneys, combine, with the Church and the foliage, and the occasional peeps of the river between the trees, and St. Katharine's hill in the back ground, to form a complete picture.

Let us enter the well kept quadrangle, or, as it is more usually termed, the court, from the direction just indicated. Leaving the high road by the little

wicket gate, crossing the green close, leaving the old walnut trees on the right
hand, across the corner of the park, we pass through the iron gate into the Hospital
premises.   We are at once impressed by the calm repose of the antiquated place,
which certainly possesses an indescribable air of its own; and, with its tall box
edgings, and old fashioned flowers, and luxuriant fig-trees, vines, and creepers, is
very unlike an ordinary college quadrangle. We begin our survey with that which
is at once the most ancient, and the most interesting, portion of the whole group.

The Church.

In the accompanying illustrations, the reader will observe four direct views of
the Church itself; two exteriors and two interiors.   They speak for themselves.
Without professing to explain them in every detail, and still less to usurp the
office of Exhibitor, it is the Master's desire, in these pages, to explain briefly what
has been done during the last eight or ten years; to direct attention to some
special points of interest; and to convey a general notion of the whole design.

The Exterior of the Church first claims our attention.   It is a massive
cruciform structure, with central tower and imposing transepts.   The west front,
with its lofty buttresses, its elegant early English double doorway ornamented
with tooth moulding, and its large decorated window, will repay an attentive survey.
Just enough of the gable-cross remains to shew that it once existed there.   The
north porch varies the line of the aisle-roof in the happiest manner; it is early
English in style, and shews the remnants of tooth-work in the door mouldings: it
is well groined, and surmounted by an upper chamber.   The windows of this and
the opposite aisle vary in character. Those nearest to the transepts are Norman, like
the lower transept-windows themselves; but the others become distinctly early
English as they approach the west.   The clerestory windows, over the tiled roofs
of the aisles, are decorated; and, together with the lead-covered roof above them,
were the work of William de Edyndon: it has been already noticed that the nave
was only thatched until his mastership. John de Campeden completed the tower
at a somewhat later period, and constructed and glazed the eight windows, two on
each side, which light the lower portion beneath the belfry.

The north transept terminates with a central buttress beneath an early English
window, and a gable-light above.   On each side of the buttress is a finely carved

CHURCH OF ST. CROSS, N.W.

No. I.

CHURCH OF ST CROSS, S.E.

No. II.

Norman window; that to the east is concealed by the ambulatory, the western one has been recently restored to its original purpose.

If the reader now passes from the first to the second external view, which is taken from the meadow behind the Hospital, he has before him the peculiar east front of the choir; with its central and side buttresses, its ten windows in different tiers, its turrets which have long lost their spires, and its circular Norman openings in the gable. A richly carved semi-Norman doorway with pointed arch,

in the wall of the north-eastern aisle, close to the transept, is now closed up. On the opposite side, in the south-east angle, is a very curious doorway, of which a sketch is annexed. This peculiar "triple arch," as it is usually called, evidently formed, in earlier times, an entrance into the Church from a cloister which then existed, and which is still to be traced in the weather tables, and in the shortening of the adjacent windows. The doorway seems to have taken its peculiar shape from the necessity of scooping into the wall on the right, in order to make the most of the scanty room allowed by a buttress in too close proximity at the left. The internal arrangement is here equally perplexing, and will be referred to presently. The roofs of the choir-aisles were lowered, and the triforium-openings glazed, in the mastership of John de Campeden. Attached to the south transept is a vaulted chamber of inferior height, which appears to have been the ancient sacristy. A considerable portion of the exterior of the Church is plastered, showing the stone work at the angles only. It has been recommended to remove this plaster, and, as far as possible, to point and restore the walls. Meanwhile, even as it is—

> "The fresh greensward and trees of various growth,
> Which planted seem where they should most adorn,
> Harmonise well with the grey masoury."

⊕⊕⊕⊕⊕⊕⊕⊕⊕⊕⊕⊕⊕⊕⊕⊕⊕⊕⊕⊕⊕⊕⊕⊕⊕⊕⊕⊕⊕⊕

THE INTERIOR of the Church now invites examination. The Master will endeavour, in the first place, to give some notion of the condition in which he found it. It was not so utterly neglected as Dr. Lewis describes in his answers to Archbishop Laud's enquiry. It was indeed in, what is called, "substantial repair;" and, as for cleanliness, it seemed to have been periodically limewashed ever since the death of that worthy Master, who signalised his reign by completing the whitewashing of the whole Church, just three weeks before he expired. The following extract from a report of the architect, in the spring of A.D. 1858, gives the true state of the case. "Internally the Church is very damp; and "it will never be otherwise until its pavements and floors have been taken up, "the soil below excavated and removed, and the pavements relaid entirely free "of it. The walls and piers generally require to be carefully cleansed from "whitewash, and the stone and purbeck marble to be everywhere exposed, and "repaired where they have been cut away. There is dry rot in some of the wooden "floors. It is quite undesirable to spend money upon a repair of the present "arrangements. A general refitting is very desirable."

At that time the floor was broken and uneven, as well as damp; the seating was of the most incongruous character, partly deal, and partly oak grained over with paint; the two lower windows at the east end were blocked up altogether; the marble shafts were limewashed; and the delicate carving coated with plaster, was in some parts actually reduced to a smooth surface. A cumbrous wooden structure, painted to resemble oak, blocked up the east end of the Church. And the general effect (such as it was) was intercepted by a high deal screen, which had been carried across the nave and aisles, and reached from the floor to the capitals of the large Norman columns. In short, the space appropriated for Divine Service was completely boxed up. Yet, in the language of the architect's report, so undesirable did it seem to spend money upon any attempted improvement of the existing arrangements, that, for some years, the Master devoted himself to his purely ministerial work; not only as the more important duty, but also, as feeling sensible that the time was not then arrived when he could deal with the Church effectually, and in a manner worthy of its high character and sacred use. It was not till A.D. 1860, that he was able fairly to begin his cherished design. But of this, more hereafter: now, for the present aspect of things.

The peculiar and indescribable charm of the Church lies in its substantial dignity and beauty of proportion. The first view which the stranger obtains, whether he enter by the north porch, or by the grand western doors, is perhaps equally good. Entering at the north, he sees the aisle and transept

INTERIOR OF THE CHURCH OF ST. CROSS LOOKING EAST.

No. 111.

arrangements to greater advantage, and he is more impressed by the grandeur of the columns. The view from the west entrance, which is depicted in the former of the two interior illustrations here given, most completely displays the extent and effect of the recent restoration. One important feature, which no past neglect could impair, is the imposing altitude and simplicity of the vaulted ceiling. Another feature is the lantern, formed out of the lower story of the central tower. But the eye instinctively rests upon the east end of the Church, where the highly enriched Norman work of De Blois is clearly visible from the west, at a distance of 125* feet. The celebrated arcading of semicircular interlacing arches, the exquisitely carved window mouldings, the purbeck shafts, now denuded of their wash, and the effective vaulting of the choir,—are all heightened in effect, and, as it were, set in a double frame, by the lofty piers and arches which support the lantern. The lantern itself is peculiarly effective, and throws an air of lightness and grace over the whole building. The corbel heads, which support the ceiling of the lantern, are very boldly designed. Nearer to the spectator, as he views the Church from the west, are the huge circular columns which bear the arches of the nave, and rest upon massive square bases. The foliated ornaments at the angles of the bases, which in continental architecture are termed "griffes," or claws, demand attention by their boldness and character. The ground plan of the Church was, no doubt, set out from the first: but, after awhile, when the work had been carried up to a certain point by its Norman architect, the western portion was suspended. The work, thus suspended, was not resumed till the transitional Norman architecture had been merged in the early English. This new style, then growing into use, was freely adopted. In some parts, the change is distinctly marked; as, for instance, in the string course, where a boss of foliage divides the Norman and early English work: but, in other places, the older style is so gradually absorbed in the new, that it is impossible to point out any precise line of demarcation. This remark is particularly applicable to the aisle-windows of the nave: the first, from the east, is distinctly Norman, with the square abacus surmounting its shafts, just like its fellows in the choir; the second is round-headed, like its Norman predecessor, but with circular abacus and later mouldings; the third is bluntly pointed; and the last window of each aisle, facing west, is distinctly early English. The great west window, which completes the work, is early decorated.

The transitional character of the architecture in the nave, from the later Norman to the more distinctly English style, to which attention has been thus

---

* The breadth of the Church is 5½ feet at the aisles, and 115 at the transepts. The height, about 57 feet to the vaulting of the nave: probably 20 feet higher to the oak ceiling of the lantern.

directed, is very characteristic of the times in which the Church was slowly built. But the choir and transepts furnish a remarkably fine specimen of the transitional style of Norman architecture itself; when the earlier Norman carving, which is sometimes of remarkable rudeness, was being succeeded by a delicacy of workmanship, combined with richness of design, which has been scarcely ever surpassed. This kind of work abounds in the choir and eastern aisles.

The projecting purbeck bases near the communion-rail, on which the chancel piers rest, seem to court inquiry; and, if cross-examined, have a tale of their own to tell. They were surmounted, till recently, by large octagonal columns of the perpendicular period. These appeared so clearly to be a later casing to earlier work, that, during the progress of the restoration, four years ago, the architect determined to investigate beneath the surface. On removing a portion of the casing, a circular column of Caen stone was found within. But some further signs of a purbeck marble capital appearing inside that again, the workmen were induced to penetrate yet deeper, and the discovery of a complete purbeck column of about twelve inches diameter, in the centre of all, was the result. An open cluster, consisting of central column and four detached shafts, all of marble, had been evidently designed in the first instance; and the sockets, for the square terminations of the shafts, are still visible on the projecting angles. But it must have become apparent, in the progress of the work, that this arrangement was not equal to the superincumbent weight; and so the northern column was at once cased with Caen stone. This material was used in the original work, but not subsequently. On trying the same experiment in the south pier, the Caen stone column was easily reached; but the workmen failed to detect the innermost shaft of marble, which led to the conclusion that the first design had been abandoned, even then. Two hundred and fifty years later, it would appear that John de Campeden considered the enlarged columns, which were nine feet six inches in circumference, still unequal to the position, and re-cased them accordingly. This remarkable discovery offered a strong temptation to recur to the primary arrangement; Mr. Butterfield, however, adopted the more prudent course; and, leaving the greater portion of De Campeden's additional casing, has restored the angular shafts, and brought the capitals into unison with the responds east and west of these central columns.

Another highly interesting incident was the discovery of the high altar slab, of dark marble, in a state of the most complete preservation. This discovery was made by the Master, before the commencement of Z. O.'s restoration, while he was engaged upon a little amateur scraping, at the east end of the Church. On the removal of the cumbrous and wholly incongruous piece of woodwork behind the communion-table, he found a large slab, eight feet three inches in length, imbedded in an upright position, in the centre of an old stone reredos, and covered with whitewash. When the wash was removed, the five crosses of consecration were found as sharply defined as when first incised. This marble slab had doubtless surmounted the high altar of alabaster, erected by John de Campeden, in the reign of Richard the Second. It now rests beneath the present table, which has been purposely constructed of the same dimensions. A smaller chantry altar slab was found, laid down as a gravestone, in the south aisle of the choir; it is considerably perished, and but two of its five crosses can now be faintly traced. This latter slab is laid down at the eastern extremity of the south aisle of the choir, in which it was found, and forms the base of the former communion table; which, with some other woodwork in the choir, was removed to this part of the Church, at the time of the recent restoration. The displaced furniture of the choir, carefully cleansed from its repeated coats of paint, is there lovingly preserved; and is in constant use, at the brethren's daily service.

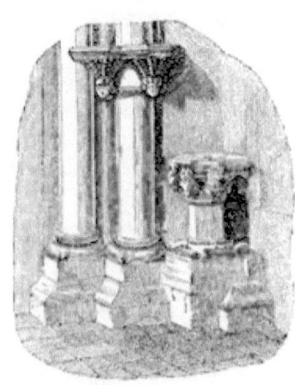

In the corresponding chapel, formed by the north aisle of the choir, considerable remains of the ancient wall-painting may be traced, on both sides, at the east end, and on the vaulting of the ceiling. Several figures are distinctly discernible. A very elegant piscina, and some brackets, of which an illustration is here given, also deserve examination. The elaborate screen, with canopy work, which divides the eastern bay of this chapel from the choir, will not fail to be noticed.

There are further interesting remnants of wall-painting, in the south transept. In a finely arched recess, in the eastern wall of this transept, once stood an altar to St. Thomas of Canterbury. The Hon. Alan Brodrick, who was at that time residing with the Master, especially undertook this portion of the work; and, as the coatings of whitewash were removed, not only did the stone carved work stand out distinctly, but, it soon became evident that, on the back of the recess, over the altar, there had been a series of pictorial representations. The outline of knights in Norman chain armour, a large sword, a mitre resting on an altar, and portions of an

I

apparently priestly figure interposing, are more or less distinctly visible.   A comparison with the larger and clearer wall-painting of the murder of à Becket, in Preston church, Brighton, materially helps to fill up the gaps; and especially, supplies the prostrate figure of the Archbishop himself, who, most provokingly, despite every effort, cannot be brought out at St. Cross.   On the south end of the same transept is a bold delineation of the taking down of our Lord from the Cross, covering the whole surface of the wall.

The recent colouring of the choir and lantern is, therefore, an attempt to reproduce a species of ornament with which the Church was, in earlier days, enriched throughout.   For this specimen of a kind of work which, till recently, had fallen so completely into disuse, we are indebted to the talent of Mr. Butterfield ;* and to the public spirit of a gentleman, "a native of Hampshire," who most munificently headed a special subscription for the purpose.   The introduction of colour is, at least, no novelty in the Church of St. Cross.   Wherever the whitewash has been removed, the remnants of ancient work of this character are discovered; and it was strongly felt, by the Architect and other friends, that any attempt at restoration, which ignored the colouring, would be unworthy of the place.

The remnants of ancient stained glass are to be found mainly in the large west window.   Its contents, however, are at present very fragmentary, and of various dates.   Mr. Winston says :—"The earliest specimens of early English glass I have "met with in the neighbourhood of Winchester, are two fragments, probably of "a border, worked in with other glass in the west window of the nave of St. Cross. "This glass belongs to the early portion of the thirteenth century, and doubtless "came out of one of the Norman windows of the Church."   He attributes the figures, now in the lower part of the window, to about the reign of Henry VI.   It is needless to say that the present arrangement is incongruous.   But it is proposed, at the earliest opportunity, to remove all the existing glass; carefully to adapt the valuable ancient glass to other windows in the Church; and then to refil the west window with the best modern glass.   The modern glass already put up is partly by Wailes, and partly by Alexander Gibbs.   The two upper windows at the east end of the choir, representing the Resurrection and Ascension, were the first presented; and are a thank offering on the part of friends who never cease to exert themselves for the improvement of the old Church, and its restoration in every part to its former beauty.   The window over the font came next.   It is an offering

---

* Mr. Butterfield's designs have been executed by Messrs. Harland and Fisher, of Southampton Street, Strand.

INTERIOR OF THE CHURCH OF ST. CROSS LOOKING WEST.

No. IV.

on the part of several young persons who had been baptized there; and possesses an interest of its own on that account. Other windows, (the gifts of various friends,) followed: each with its own history and interest.

The pavement of encaustic tiles deserves especial notice. This has been already referred to in an earlier portion of the book, as the work of John de Campeden in the fourteenth century. But, owing to burials, alterations, and the repaving effected by Dr. Lewis in the seventeenth century, the main design had become entirely obliterated; and even the lesser patterns had been quite neglected. All the old tiles have now been relaid, with due regard to pattern, in the north and south aisles. They rest upon a pavement of York stone, beneath which there is complete ventilation. The nave and choir are laid with new tiles, carefully prepared by Minton, from the old designs: the only new pattern being the mystic letters of the munificent benefactor, "Z.O."

In the eastern wall of the south transept, close to the present organ, is the somewhat perplexing inner arrangement of the "triple arch;" of which an illustration is here given. It was unquestionably an entrance, in early times. On clearing out the odds and ends, (capitals and other pieces of columns, with the colour still adhering to them; fragments of a broken piscina, etc.,) with which it had been blocked up, the old tile pavement was found at the bottom. But whether, at a later date, the pieces were worked up without design; or whether it may have been employed for the distribution of some dole, or alms; the writer does not

profess to decide. The incomplete arch above it, is ornamented with the double potent, a device supposed to be taken from the armorial bearings of the Founder. The peculiar construction beneath it, whereby the flat heading of the original doorway is planned with a key-stone, on the principle of an arch, deserves attention. A similar construction is observable in the flat-headed doorway in the north aisle of the choir.

The triforium-arrangements, and wall-galleries, are very complete throughout the Church. In some parts, from their coloured ornamentation, and their extra width, they bear evidence of having been once in frequent use.   In the foregoing description, the Master has purposely abstained from touching upon many objects of interest and value, which the visitor will at once see for himself, or, which the intelligent Exhibitor will explain.   He cannot bring this general notice of the present aspect of his grand old Church to a conclusion, nor can he reflect on the striking contrast it presents to what met the eye some ten years ago, without a hearty ascription of praise to God, Who has put it into the hearts of so many of His servants to give freely of their substance to adorn and beautify His holy House.

BEAUFORT'S TOWER, REFECTORY, AND MASTER'S RESIDENCE.

A few preliminary remarks upon the position of the Hospital-buildings may be acceptable.   The general plan consists of an outer and inner quadrangle.   The entrance to the former is on the north side of the Hospital, and presents no special architectural features.   On the east side of the entrance court is what is commonly known as "the Hundred Mennes' Hall," now converted into a brewhouse.   On the west are the kitchen and stabling.   On the south are Beaufort's tower and two bays of the Refectory.   Thence, passing through the gateway, the visitor reaches the inner court in which the Church is situated.

Illustrations v and vi give slightly varied views of the noble tower and gate-house erected by Cardinal Beaufort.   They are taken from the south, facing the Church. Over the arch is seen a square-headed and transomed two-light window, belonging to the muniment room; and above this a single vacant niche, which is said to have contained a statue of the Virgin.*   The opposite side of the tower, facing the outer court, is adorned with three canopied niches: in one of which is the kneeling figure of Beaufort, in his Cardinal's hat and robes.   The two remaining niches are

---

* Milner, writing in A.D. 1798, says—"This was filled with a female statue, until within the last fifty "years; when it fell down by accident, and was destroyed.   The venerable brethren, who remembered this "occurrence, and the risk which one of their number ran of being killed by its falling upon him, said that it "represented a milk-maid with a pail upon her head; and that the original foundation of the Hospital by "De Blois was owing to his meeting with a person of that description on this spot, and to the conversation "which he had with her upon the utility of such a charity.   We do not hesitate to pronounce that this "supposed milk-maid, with the pail upon her head, was intended for the blessed Virgin, with her high crown, "as seen in many of her statues: and we have, in this fabricated history, a curious instance of the stories that "were sometimes palmed off upon ignorant iconoclasts, in order to preserve religious statues."

BEAUFORT'S TOWER AND REFECTORY, ST. CROSS.

No. V.

empty. It is conjectured that one contained the statue of the first Founder, and that the central niche held the holy Cross, in commemoration of which the Hospital was dedicated. Beneath is the principal entrance. The archway is four-centred, and well moulded; and in the spandrils are the royal arms of England, and those of the Cardinal. The latter are distinguished here, and in other places, by a border surrounding the shield. The moulding above the arch bears the Cardinal's hat, together with the heads (it is suggested) of John of Gaunt, his father; of his royal nephews, Henry V and Henry VI; and of his predecessor Wykeham. The gateway is vaulted and ribbed. On the east side is the porter's lodge. The gates themselves are strictly closed and barred, by the porter, at nine in the evening in summer, and at eight in winter: after which hour there is neither egress nor ingress without the Master's permission. Little hardship is felt in this respect. The brethren keep very primitive hours, remembering the old adage,

> "EARLY to bed, and early to rise,
> Makes a man healthy, wealthy, and wise."

THE Refectory adjoins the tower on the west side. Externally it is distinguished, from the domestic buildings beyond it, by its bold porch and flight of steps, and by its three perpendicular transomed windows, with intervening buttresses. In summer and autumn, it is further enriched with the luxuriant foliage of fig-trees, and the variegated hues of a Virginian creeper; which, in combination with the architectural details, enhance the general effect. Internally, although in a rougher state than might be wished, it conveys a good idea of a banqueting hall in the olden time. It is forty-five feet in length, twenty-four feet in breadth, and thirty-two feet in height, to the apex of the rafters. An open hearth occupies the centre of the chamber, after the fashion of an earlier age; and around the glowing embers of this central fire the ancient brethren still quaff their ale and sing their songs on Gaudy-days. Occasions of this sort carry us back to days when, perhaps, the old walls resounded more frequently to the ringing laugh, or the jocund song; and again, to the times succeeding the Restoration of the Monarchy, when the "bottles of sack" formed a somewhat important item in the steward's account. The minstrels' gallery remains over the entrance screen.

> "MERRY it is in halle to hear the harpe,
> The minstrelles synge, the jogelours carpe."

But the chief feature is the fine open-timbered roof, which is in good preservation. It is in four bays; and has not, like most of the other woodwork, been painted white.

There is no wall-wainscotting remaining in the hall, except at the upper end, where the raised dais and high table continue as in days of yore. This end of the hall is enriched with a curious and valuable specimen of an ancient Flemish triptych, of which an outline is here given.

It represents the holy family in the central compartment; and, on either side, St. Katharine and St. Barbara. The latter is distinguished by a tower, in which her father Dioscorus, a heathen of Hierapolis, is said to have immured her. St. Katharine is known by the wheel provided for her execution, and by a sword in her left hand. This painting on panel has been attributed to Albert Dürer. There is, however, no conclusive evidence of its authorship; nor of the circumstances under which it came into the possession of the Hospital. Of its real excellence a connoisseur thus writes: — "The triptych in the refectory at St. Cross, to my small experience, seems one of the most beautiful pictures extant."*

The original stained glass, in the upper lights of the windows, deserves notice. The royal arms are represented bordered, and surmounted by the Cardinal's hat, from which depend the strings and tassels. The words of the surrounding motto are "a honor et lyesse."

---

* A similar painting, on very old oak, has been for generations preserved in the family of the Rev. A. Earle, Vicar of West Alvington, Devon. He describes the side figures and central composition as identical; but the back-ground as different. His picture, he says, has always been considered to be a Lucas Cranach. This eminent German painter was a contemporary of Albert Dürer. He was born in A.D. 1472, and died in A.D. 1553.

BEAUFORT'S TOWER AND AMBULATORY, ST. CROSS.

No. VI.

W. SAVAGE, PHOT.

It has been already remarked, in the first part of this book, that the present rough staircase to the muniment room, which so materially interferes with the dais, is not the original arrangement.* It lessens the space available for the high table; and for that reason has been found somewhat inconvenient when the ancient hall has been used for those purposes of hospitality for which it was originally constructed. A brief reference to a few of these festive occasions may interest the reader.

On the 11th June, A.D. 1855, being the feast of St. Barnabas, the present Master entertained the brethren and some personal friends at dinner in the hall, for the first time. On a subsequent occasion of this kind, the then Lord Mayor of London† honoured the Master and brethren with his company at dinner, and was pleased to compliment their bowl of punch. On the 10th of March, A.D. 1863, the brethren and all the inmates dined with the Master and his family in hall, to celebrate the wedding of the Prince and Princess of Wales. A month afterwards, on the occasion of opening the new Organ, April 11th, the late Bishop of Rochester,‡ and a very large party of gentry and clergy of the county and neighbourhood, lunched in the old Refectory of Cardinal Beaufort. But the largest and most influential gathering of the kind was on the 19th October, A.D. 1865, at the re-opening of the Church, which had been closed for more than twelve months during the progress of the restoration. After the opening service, and sermon by the Bishop of Winchester, the old hall was filled with guests in every part; and the social meal was followed by some excellent and genial speeches. The Bishop presided; § and was supported by the Master and a large number of influential residents in the diocese, including Lord Eversley, Sir William and Lady Heathcote, Mr. Melville and Lady Charlotte Portal, Mr. Sclater-Booth, M.P., Mr. Beach, M.P., Mr. Simonds, M.P., the Archdeacons of Winchester and Surrey,‖ and considerably more than one hundred of the gentry and clergy. The next day, the hall was equally full of the village school-children, who had their separate treat. And the day following, the Master, supported by the Ven. James Randall, Archdeacon of Berks, and several personal friends and relatives, entertained the brethren themselves, for whom, on the two previous days there had been no room in their own hall. And again, since "the Winchester

---

* "The primitive ladders, by which formerly the solars, or upper chambers, were approached, were now "discarded for staircases of a goodly size, flanked with curiously carved banisters of oak."—*Parker's Domestic Architecture of England in XV. Century.*

† Mr. Alderman Carter.   ‡ Dr. Wigram.

§ Seated under a rich canopy, emblazoned with the arms of the See, prepared and presented by Mr. Francis Joseph Baigent.

‖ The Venerable Dean of Winchester would have been present, but for the death of Viscount Palmerston, which occurred the previous day.

Church Choral Union" has held its annual festival of parish choirs in the Church of St. Cross, the hall has proved of essential use for dining the choirs between the services.

On ordinary occasions, the brethren assemble in hall to receive their hot dinners, on Sundays, Mondays, Tuesdays, and Thursdays, at twelve o'clock : and after grace has been said, and the meat carved, each brother is accustomed to carry his share to his own room. At eight o'clock each morning in the summer, and at nine in winter, the brothers assemble in hall for their daily allowance of beer. They generally appear in good time, with beer-can in hand, each wearing his gown and cross. And it is pleasant to hear their morning salutations, or to see them chatting in little groups on the porch steps, waiting till the bell summons them into hall. Under the hall is a crypt, with a central shaft supporting its vaulted roof : this makes an excellent beer cellar.

Beyond the hall, and approached by a sloping passage, is the Hospital KITCHEN, a fine, lofty room, furnished with every convenience for cooking on a large scale ; not with the now almost universal closed range, but with a huge open grate, of ample size to roast a whole sheep, if required.

Next to the hall is the MASTER'S RESIDENCE, which is spacious and convenient, with a very pleasant entrance hall, partially panelled in oak. The rooms on the principal floor are large and lofty ; and the long corridors, with deeply recessed casements in the thickness of the wall, some of them ornamented with the remains of ancient painted glass, have a singular air of quaintness and antiquity. Some of the windows have been enlarged, at a comparatively recent period ; but, with this exception, it presents externally precisely the same peculiar features as the portion now appropriated to the brethren, out of which it has evidently been constructed, at a period subsequent to the original building.*

THE ROOMS OF THE BRETHREN.

THESE occupy the west side of the quadrangle. Their external aspect is well represented in the two accompanying views, marked IX and X. The long range of roof, covering the refectory, the Master's residence, and the brothers' rooms, is carried from Beaufort's tower round the north and west sides of the inner court at

* Dolman, in his " Examples of Ancient Domestic Architecture," remarks :—"On careful examination of " the plans, the author has ascertained that were the buildings completely restored,—(the Master's House and " other portions, as they at present exist, indicating considerable departure from the original arrangement,)— " there is accommodation for exactly the number of inmates provided by Cardinal Beaufort."

BROTHERS' ROOMS, ST. CROSS.

No. IX.

the same level : but the monotony of this arrangement is pleasantly varied by the chimneys. The design of this portion of the building is exceedingly simple, and consists of square-headed windows without tracery, low arched doorways, and a range of chimney-projections with high octagonal shafts. Each dwelling comprises a sitting room, bed room, scullery, and closet, and is very compactly planned. The back closets are externally arranged as a series of gabled projections towards the gardens; and, like the chimneys on the other side, very happily vary the otherwise unbroken line of the elevation. The Lockburn, a clear and rapidly flowing watercourse, conveyed from the river Itchen, to which it returns at some distance from the buildings, runs beneath these projections, and immediately carries off all impurities. This sanitary arrangement is simple and effective.

Before any restoration was commenced in the Church, the attention of the Master and Trustees was directed to this portion of the building, and to the increased comfort of the aged inmates. Two sets of rooms, one on the ground floor and one above, were, at a considerable cost, fitted up as model rooms. In the other sets, where less costly improvements were effected, stone sinks were placed in the sculleries, and ranges with ovens in the sitting rooms, for all who were desirous to have them. The outer doors, opening to the quadrangle, were in a most unsatisfactory condition : in two cases, oak doors of substantial workmanship and handsome design have been already substituted. The pent-house coverings over these outer doors are in worse condition than the doors themselves; and only remain until they can be replaced by some better arrangement. The central doorway of the seven leads to the common pump, and to the garden allotments of the fraternity. The brothers take the most lively interest in their garden, which has a good wall, and is very productive.

THE AMBULATORY.

On the east side of the quadrangle is an exceedingly picturesque range of buildings, which unites that portion of the structure adjacent to Beaufort's tower, with the Church. These buildings comprise a covered way, or ambulatory,* communicating directly with the north transept of the Church; and a gallery above, divided into a series of narrow chambers opening into each other. It has been conjectured

* This existing ambulatory is totally distinct from the ancient southern cloister, which once communicated with the opposite transept, and connected the Church with buildings which have disappeared centuries ago.

K

that the gallery formed part of the Hospital infirmary. This, however, may admit of considerable doubt.

At Thornbury Castle, Gloucestershire, there was a passage arrangement, of cloister below and gallery above, leading to the church. A short quotation from " Parker's domestic Architecture of England " may interest the reader, and throw some light upon the subject. He describes—"A fair cloister, or walk, paved with " brick, over which is a fair large gallery leading to the parish church of Thornbury, " at the end whereof is a room with a chimney, and a window looking into the said " church, where the Duke (of Buckingham) sometimes used to hear service in the " same church."

That the gallery at St. Cross, as well as the ambulatory, was used for a communication with the Church is beyond doubt; for the window at the end of it had been cut and altered into a passage-way leading into another gallery inside the Church, and extending all across the north transept. The clearest evidence of the former existence of such an inner gallery was found, at the time of the recent restoration, by the fact that the stonework had been cut away at regular intervals to receive the timbers which supported it. The height of this gallery, and of the wooden structure or second gallery which covered it, is still marked by two stone corbels, one immediately above the other, in the wall of the north transept, between the end windows. From this inner gallery the large wall-painting of the descent from the Cross, at the end of the opposite transept, must have been distinctly visible. It is not improbable that the painting was expressly designed and executed for the benefit of those who once occupied this position. The second illustration gives the inner view of the ambulatory. On the right, is the door of the turret staircase leading to the gallery. On the left, is the entrance to the Master's garden.

It has been already stated that all this portion of the buildings may be attributed to Master Robert Sherborne, at the beginning of the sixteenth century. He has left his initials and motto over the fire-places, in the porter's lodge, and in the chamber above it, and around the quaint pillar which supports the little oriel which forms a prominent feature in the view. This custom of introducing the initials of the builder had become general at that period.

THE PARK, MEADOWS, AND GARDENS.

IMMEDIATELY south of the Hospital, and separated only by a dwarf wall and iron railing, on the site of the former buildings which were pulled down by Dr. Lockman

AMBULATORY, ST. CROSS.

No. VII.

W. SAVAGE PHOT.

AMBULATORY, INTERIOR, ST. CROSS.

No. VIII.

in the last century, is a spacious meadow called the Park. It is well studded with trees, and reaches to the banks of the Itchen. The footpath to Twyford crosses the park. An extensive rookery is being gradually formed here: the birds first began to build thirteen years ago, and have added to the number of their nests year by year ever since. When the grass is mown the haymakers claim a "jack of beer" from the Hospital, which is provided by immemorial custom. The accompanying view happened to be taken at an interesting, and sometimes an exciting, moment. A tree had fallen, or had been cut down. When such an event occurs, the brethren are entitled to the top and lop; and the whole community is astir until the fallen hero is dismembered, and his leafy spoils equally divided. Some of the brothers fall to work vigorously for themselves; others, from age or inexperience, act by deputy; but the oldest and most infirm members of the fraternity survey the field of action, if they can do no more than offer advice; and, at last, the senior brother decides that the lots are fairly apportioned. This decision being acquiesced in, the next thing is to convey the lots to their own wood-stores; and the two Hospital barrows are in great requisition. The Master has often seen an aged brother on these occasions shouldering a huge log which, even allowing that it could be brought within the category of "top and lop," seemed almost too great a weight for four-score and over. But it is astonishing what fresh youth old limbs can assume at times like these.

Divided from the park by a low fence, and to be recognised (in the accompanying view) by the headstones beyond it, is the quiet little cemetery; wherein many of the brothers rest from their labours, in the blessed hope of a joyful resurrection. It is a peaceful, bright, and sunny spot; and is endeared to the living occupants of the Hospital as the hallowed resting-place, not only of the long-buried dead of past generations, but of personal friends whom they have known and loved. Perhaps nothing presents a truer test of the changed and improved tone of feeling amongst the brethren, than the ideas they cherish in regard to this little church-yard. Thirteen years ago no burial had taken place in it within the memory of living men. Some brothers were buried in St. Faith's ground; a few in a little plot eastward of the Church; some were carried to the Winchester cemetery; still more seem to have been taken to the places whence they came: and the present Master remembers well, when he first came, being intrusted by more than one brother with directions as to the prospective place of his interment, elsewhere. There had been widely prevalent an unsettled and uncomfortable feeling in respect to their abode while living; and dying they had no wish to leave their bones in a place which they had scarcely felt to be their real home. But the "long winter of their discontent" was drawing to a close; elements of discord no longer existed to disturb the harmony of the place; the senior brother (Charles Matthews), who died just at that time, expressed a wish that he should be buried on the spot; and now, for the burial of an inmate to take place elsewhere, is a rare exception. There is no wish, on the part of the brethren, to be separated in death from a spot where they have passed the closing days of life in freedom from worldly anxieties, and in peaceful preparation for their expected change. (Job xiv. 14.)

The footpath to the east of the Church leads the pedestrian, from the park through "pigeon-house mead," in the direction of Winchester College. This meadow derives its name from a very large pigeon-house which formerly stood at the north-east corner of the Master's garden, but is now only to be traced in a semicircular bend of the garden-wall at that corner. From the next stile northward, a very good view is obtained of the Church, and a portion of the Hospital buildings, including Beaufort's tower. This constitutes the concluding view here presented. The landscape is enhanced by the intervening foliage of the garden, which lies to the east of the ambulatory, and is described, in the early part of the last century, during the rule of Dr. Markland, as adorned with evergreens and watered by a canal. It is spacious and fruitful; and capable of great improvement when circumstances permit.

It will be remembered that some of the meadows and closes immediately adjacent to the Hospital had been leased out, in the reign of Queen Elizabeth, to the great inconvenience of the Master and brethren. Since then, the home property has always been kept in hand, or let from year to year at its proper value, for the due maintenance of the establishment.

The reader has now been conducted through the Hospital-buildings, and around the contiguous premises; he has surveyed the gardens, and walked in the park; he can still stroll, if he please, under the shade of the elms and along the smooth bank of the beautiful Itchen, as far as the water-mill. And after he has seen the swans; and refreshed himself, on his return, with travellers' fare at the porter's lodge; he may like to ask some questions as to the future prospects of the Institution.

VIEW FROM THE PARK, ST. CROSS.

No. XI.

VIEW FROM THE MEADOW, ST. CROSS.

No. XII.

PART III.

Restoration and Future Prospects.

"Is there no pledge to hope's fore-seeing eye,
Which these firm walls and living courts supply?
No bard can find a ruined oriel here
On which to muse, and shed the pensive tear.
No moss-grown stones, no ivied loop-holes, lend
Thoughts such as poets love to weave and blend.
But here the days of Restitution dawn,
Here gleams are seen of the millenial morn.
Times of refreshing mark this favoured spot,
Though dark the providence which cast the lot."

ENOUGH has been written in these pages to show that the PAST HISTORY of St. Cross is replete with interesting recollections. It is interwoven with the biography of men, who in their day took a leading part in the ecclesiastical and civil government of our country. Its PRESENT ASPECT has been also described. Calm and peaceful, though the subject of so much strife and litigation; neat and well ordered, though for the time straitened to the utmost as to pecuniary resources; never more active than when most seriously reduced in circumstances; and shooting out the more vigorously when cut down to the very roots.

What, then, are its FUTURE PROSPECTS? After thirteen years of battle with the difficulties of the situation, sometimes patiently waiting his time, but more frequently struggling to surmount the obstacles presented by crippled resources, the writer has abated none of his hopes for the future. He has not a doubt that St. Cross is destined, in the providence of God, to be far more extensively useful than it ever yet has been; and that it will be made to realise, in a much greater degree, the benevolent designs of its noble Founders. The question is, whether he and his co-trustees can reasonably hope themselves to witness this happy consummation? Time is required. Not merely time to mature wise plans;

but, especially in this instance, time to allow leases to fall in, and financial difficulties to right themselves. From the nature of the case, as will presently be explained more fully, it is a race of lives against lives; and many of the lives upon the existing leases are comparatively quite young. Meanwhile, they who can hardly hope to behold the consummation may live to see the dawn, they who cannot expect to complete the edifice may lay the foundation, and plan the superstructure. At least, each year is bringing the day of restitution nearer; and rendering it more important for the friends and managers of St. Cross to be prepared with well digested measures for the future.

THE PROVISIONAL SCHEME FOR MANAGEMENT.

THE circumstances under which St. Cross came before the Court of Chancery have been already stated. A "Scheme for the interim management of the Hospital," was approved by the Court, on the 22nd June, A.D. 1855; and slightly modified on the 20th March, A.D. 1857. It is expressly stated that "this Scheme "is intended to be a temporary one; and shall in no way prejudice the claims of "the Almshouse of Noble Poverty." And that, "when, by the falling in of the "existing leases of the charity property, or otherwise, the income shall be increased "to a sum which, in the opinion of Her Majesty's Attorney-General, shall make it "desirable that a new or further Scheme should be settled for the due administra- "tion of the charity, application shall be made to the Court for that purpose."

1. It is one of the main features of the Scheme, which it shares in common with other schemes for the regulation of similar charities,* that "The charity, and the property thereof, shall be under the management and control of Trustees."† The duties of the Trustees, as to the charity property, are thus defined. "The

---

* Compare, for instance, a "Scheme for the management and regulation of the Hospital of God, in "Greatham, in the county palatine of Durham;" approved by the High Court of Chancery, 31st July, 1866."

† The present Trustees are—

"lands and buildings of the charity, except the buildings within the precincts of
"the Hospital, shall from time to time be let and demised at the best annual rent
"or rents that can reasonably be obtained for the same; either from year to year,
"or for any term or number of years not exceeding twenty-one years in possession,
"and not in reversion; and without taking any fine, or premium, on the making
"of any such demise."

This clause furnishes an opportunity for giving a brief explanation of the
present impoverished circumstances of the Hospital; and of the reason why, with
large revenues in prospective, the present administrators of the charity have to deal
with such straitened resources. The main source of income to previous Masters
was derived from the enormous fines which were paid on the renewal of leases of the
Hospital property for three lives. And the annual rents, reserved for the
maintenance of the Hospital, and payable during the continuance of the leases,
were small in proportion. The larger the fine, the smaller the rent. But the late
Master renewed leases on these terms, and received his fines, to the very last moment;
leaving the present managers of the Institution the burden of paying the heavy
remainder of chancery costs, (amounting to many thousands sterling,) and of
maintaining the existing establishment on an efficient footing, with no income whatever beyond what is received from these reserved rents. Under such circumstances,
and with such additional liabilities, one or two fines would have been of the
greatest value. But any such renewal was absolutely forbidden by the Court, that
there might be no further impediment to the earliest possible expiration of the old
leases. And not only was Beaufort's advowson of Crondall sold, to aid in paying
off the costs, but a large sum of money was borrowed for the same purpose.*

The gross amount of annual income was returned to the Trustees, soon after
their appointment, at £1722 : 2 : 4. This has been recently increased to the

* The following is a brief summary of costs, drawn up in July, A. D. 1857 :—

	£	s	d	£	s	d
Attorney-General, to August 1st, 1853	2959	5	4			
Ditto, subsequently	1150	0	0			
				4109	5	4
Injunction against Mr. Holloway				711	16	4
Surveyor's charges				1793	2	6
Costs of the Bishop, to August 1st, 1853	419	3	1			
Ditto, subsequently	280	0	0			
				699	3	1
Costs of Master and Brethren				350	0	0
				7663	7	5
Already paid on Account				1997	5	3
Then remaining to be paid				£5666	2	2

extent of about £200 per annum, by the falling in of the lease of the tithe rent-charge of Freefolk. But it has not been materially enlarged from other sources; and, as the present yearly expenditure (including interest of money borrowed to pay costs, repairs, and other necessary outgoings incident to the nature of the Hospital-property,) is about £1800, or rather more, it will be obvious that the margin of surplus revenue is exceedingly scanty. The lease of the Freefolk tithes, which has just fallen in, was granted upon a term of years: but all the other leases having been granted upon three lives, and continuing in force so long as any one of the three survives, there are no means of ascertaining with precision when the revenues of the charity will be further increased. The estimated annual value of the property, when the leases shall have all fallen in, considerably exceeds £8000.*

2. The next portion of the Scheme relates to the Master: his appointment, stipend, authority, and duties. These are points on which he feels it is unnecessary, perhaps unbecoming, for him to enlarge in a work of this character. Suffice it to say that the emoluments of the office are scarcely equal to its prestige. The present stipend is avowedly proportioned rather to the diminished means of the charity, than to the duties imposed, or the position to be maintained.

3. The conclusion of the Scheme deals with the brethren, and the hundred-hall poor. The brethren are to receive their usual rations; a weekly payment in money, of five shillings each; and their cloth gowns yearly. But the Trustees have an option, "if they shall think fit, to abolish the system of supplying "them with food, etc.; and they shall, in such case, pay to each brother a certain "fixed stipend, not less than £30 per annum, and not exceeding £40 per annum, by "weekly instalments, in lieu of all such allowances and payments, excepting the "gowns as aforesaid." The brethren are maintained at De Blois' original number of "thirteen." They are to be poor and impotent men, having attained the age of fifty years at the least, and not in receipt of parochial relief. The hundred-hall-poor are continued "for the present," far below their ancient number. But here, likewise, the intention is to order things on a more liberal scale, whenever funds permit.

The property of "Noble Poverty," remains distinguishable, to a great extent from the original endowments of St. Cross, and it is the expressed design of the Court to settle a scheme for the revival of that portion of the charity, when, by the falling in of the existing leases, or otherwise, there shall be an available income sufficient to render such a step desirable.

---

* As valued by Mr. Tite, M.P., £8052 17s. 11d.

Brother Whitehead. Brother King. Brother Piper. Brother Griffiths.

W. SAVAGE, PHOT.

GROUP OF BRETHREN, ST. CROSS.

No. XIII.

FIRST ATTEMPTS AT RESTORING THE CHURCH.

For the reasons just assigned, the present Master was debarred, at his entrance upon office, from attempting the enlargement of the brotherhood, or the revival of Noble Poverty, or any permanent extension of the charity. And, after he had worked up his congregation, and organised the parish of St. Faith, he had absolutely no practicable work left him, in the immediate exercise of his office, but to restore the magnificent Church of the Hospital. If this could be rescued from neglect, and, by voluntary contributions, restored to its original beauty, in readiness for the enlargement of the Institution, one important point would be gained in anticipation.

The success has been beyond his hopes. And, beyond the immediate success, a good beginning of a greater work has been made. The successful restoration of the Church is, in itself, an augury of the successful restoration, in the end, of the whole design so nobly planned by Beaufort and De Blois. What has been already accomplished, in the teeth of obstacles, is an omen of more important achievements in store, when all those obstacles are removed. For it must become the duty and privilege of the Master and Trustees, at some future day (more or less distant), with the advice and sanction of the higher court, to remodel the Institution itself, and to place it in a position worthy of the benevolent intentions of its munificent Founders.

It is true, the time is not yet. But so it seemed a few years ago with regard to the restoration of the fabric. The condition of the Church thirteen years back has been described. A few minor improvements were effected; but the Master felt that he could do nothing material, perhaps ought not under the circumstances to attempt anything, without the co-operation of the future Trustees. For their appointment he waited (somewhat impatiently) two years. His own institution took place April 16th, A.D. 1855: and the first meeting of the newly-appointed Trustees was held on April 14th, A.D. 1857. During that interval, all who were interested in St. Cross, both inside and out, were longing for the appointment of the Trustees. Their advent was to inaugurate a new state of things. This was the panacea for all the ills and wrongs of the place; and well does the Master

L

remember one of the ancient brethren who, as death was approaching, expressed his deep concern that he might not live to see this desired consummation. Those, however, who were spared to hail the appointment of the Trustees, and to welcome their first arrival, scarcely realised the immediate advantages they had been too eagerly expecting. Much necessary business had to be transacted. The real state of the case was officially explained. It became still more apparent that there were no surplus funds : and that, with the utmost economy, it would be impossible for years, to pay the remaining chancery costs, still amounting to £5666.

What could be done? How was a Restoration to be even so much as named? To start a subscription seemed the only chance left. The Master accordingly wrote to the Trustees at some length, inviting them to join him in heading a subscription list, to be circulated through the county, with a statement of the circumstances under which such a step was taken. The replies to this preliminary and private application, on the part of the Master to his co-trustees, were not encouraging. The noblemen and gentlemen, upon whose judgment he most relied, pointed out to him, with much force, the difficulty of making such an appeal in a case like this, where the property really existed, and would eventually fall in to the Hospital ; though, for the time, it was incapable of being touched. They advised him to wait. He had no other course left. Though he feared he might wait till the next century ; and, even then, be informed that the restoration of the Church was not the special object for which the funds of the charity were applicable.

Compelled, in this way, to abandon the idea of any large or comprehensive work, his attention was devoted from time to time, to such smaller matters as were conducive to the convenience of the congregation, or the more decent performance of Divine Service. For instance, the seating was partially re-arranged ; the children were transferred to the north transept, where a small organ had been introduced ; and, early in the year A.D. 1860, the Master felt that, with an increased and increasing number of communicants, a more adequate supply of Communion plate had become an indispensable requisite. The then existing service consisted of nothing but a small-sized paten and chalice, and a silver plate of later date : the last mentioned having been presented by Bishop Porteus, apparently as an alms-dish. There was no provision for the separation of the consecrated and unconsecrated elements ; and the single chalice was no longer large enough for its purpose, without being replenished. The question suggested itself :—" Would Lord Guilford, after the example of his predecessor, Bishop Porteus, leave a pleasant memorial of his long connection with the place, and present a chalice as a further supplement to the Hospital plate?" The idea was respectfully communicated to his lordship: but with what success the following reply reveals :—"Deprived of my rights, as I have been by the Court of Chancery, I am perhaps the very last person to whom application should be made for a donation to the Hospital. The heavy debt you mention would not exist, had not the Master of the Rolls forced me from my office, and deprived the Corporation of its chartered property, and placed it in other hands. To those hands I must refer you. Waldershare, February 16th, A.D. 1860." The Master met with greater success in other quarters. The Visitor, the Trustees, and the congregation, liberally responded to his appeal; and the present very handsome and costly service of Communion plate, partly old and partly new,* is the result. One of the Trustees, to whose judicious counsel and liberal aid, on all occasions, the Master is most deeply indebted, Sir William Heathcote, made the remark that, "this was worth doing well, inasmuch as it might be considered the first step in the much desired restoration." His words were quickly realised: for, in a very short time, before the end of that year, the thorough repair of the nave of the Church was actually commenced.

The first attempt at anything approaching to a thorough restoration was brought about in this way.—By strict economy, during the four or five preceding years, a sum of about six hundred pounds had been accumulated, after the ordinary expenses of the Hospital were defrayed. The amount raised by the sale of the Crondall advowson, in addition to a previous sum of £838 applicable to the same purpose, had materially diminished the chancery costs; and had indeed completely discharged that portion which required immediate payment. It was stated that the Attorney-General would not press for the discharge of the remaining sum, which related to his own costs. And the Trustees resolved, after some hesitation, to apply their surplus, not towards the liquidation of the debt, but to the somewhat urgent needs of the Church.

It was proposed by the Architect to begin with the NAVE, as being that portion of the Church least in use at the time, and yet most capable of being rendered available for an enlarged congregation in future. By a judicious expenditure of the sum in hand, the nave and its aisles were completely cleansed from their repeated coats of whitewash; the entire flooring was relaid, free of the earth, partly in oak, and partly in York stone; the decayed doors, (north, west,

---

* Adapted and designed by Mr. Butterfield, and prepared by Keith, of the City Road, London.

and south,) were replaced in oak, after the original patterns; and the whole was made ready for use, except relaying the ancient tiles upon the stone-bedding, and covering the oak floor with suitable seats.

LACK OF FUNDS.—AN UNEXPECTED AND UNKNOWN BENEFACTOR.

AT this critical point the work ceased for a season. Not only was the balance in hand expended; but the Attorney-General thought the time had arrived for the payment in full of his outstanding costs. For this purpose, it was found necessary to borrow considerably more than £2000, at a rate sufficiently high to pay off principal as well as interest in thirty years. And the additional annual payment thus necessitated, by absorbing the surplus income, at once extinguished all reasonable hope of going forward with the restoration, so far prosperously commenced. Yet, notwithstanding these delays, after a pause of two or three years, the work was resumed with renewed vigour in the Spring of A.D. 1864, in consequence of a very remarkable and munificent offer on the part of an unexpected Benefactor.

Meanwhile, the Master and his immediate friends were not idle. In the Autumn of A.D. 1861, the Norman work at the east end of the Church was partially opened out, and the heavy deal screen removed. About the same time the upper stained glass windows were given. In A.D. 1862-3, the fine organ, by Walker, was built and erected. And in the Summer and Autumn of the latter year, brother King, with the help and direction of the Honourable Alan Brodrick and the Master, was continually at work on small and accessible portions of the building; picking out plaster, scraping off whitewash, and revealing one after another those delicacies of detail which form one of the chief attractions of the architecture of the transition period.

In the midst of this gradual progress, on the morning of the 15th of August, a most unlooked-for letter arrived, from an anonymous and wholly unknown writer. It was posted from Cowes; and addressed to the Master. The writer stated that, in a recent visit to St. Cross, he had been much impressed by the beauty of the Church, and had heard with regret that the work of restoration was delayed from the want of available funds. He proceeded to offer a donation of £500, on certain specified conditions. These were to the following effect :—that the sum so given should be expended on the east end of the Church : that the lower windows should be filled with stained glass, corresponding in treatment and colour with those already inserted above : that there should be some memorial in the glass, of the Queen and of the late Prince Consort, and of the Bishop and Master for the time being : and further, that any ancient glass, or tiles, displaced during the work, should be carefully preserved in appropriate situations. The writer subscribed himself " Z.O.," and requested an answer to be forwarded to the General Post Office, London.

The Master and Trustees most thankfully accepted so liberal an offer; and the money was most promptly paid. But, strange to say, although the same munificent benefactor has subsequently given a sum of £250 more, " Z.O." is, to this hour, as completely shrouded in mystery, as on the day when the first letter was laid on the Master's breakfast-table at St. Cross.

RESUMPTION AND PROGRESS OF THE WORK.

THE CHOIR was now to be the scene of operation; and Mr. Butterfield was again busy with examinations and plans. It soon became evident that £500 would but partially do the required work, even if limited to the eastern end. And the Master was naturally most anxious to make full use of this excellent opportunity ; and, while the scaffolding was in the Church, to carry on the restoration, so as to include the lantern and transepts also, and thus to clear off the whitewash throughout the whole interior of the building. It was resolved that the whole of " Z.O's." donation should be spent in actual work; the Hospital defraying the Architect's commission. This was the utmost that the charity funds could then allow.

Clearly the time had now arrived to make an appeal to the County. The circumstance of an entire stranger having come forward so nobly, justified, and almost compelled, an attempt to raise a sum sufficient to carry out the work, thus recommenced, with some degree of completeness. The appeal was made ; and proved very successful. All the Trustees responded. The Bishop gave a handsome donation of £110. And the Wandering Minstrels gave one of their admirable concerts, which produced £138, clear of expenses, for the restoration fund.

On the 30th of April, A.D. 1864, the agreement was signed for doing the first portion of the work. On the 26th of the following November, the Bishop, and a large party of county gentlemen, lunched with the Master, and inspected the progress of the works. And on Thursday, October 19th, A.D. 1865, the restored Church was re-opened for Divine Service. On this occasion the Bishop was again present, and preached a most appropriate sermon from Haggai ii, 9 :—"The glory " of this latter House shall be greater than of the former, saith the Lord of Hosts : "and in this place will I give peace, saith the Lord of Hosts."

The next day Mr. Melville Portal, of Laverstoke House, who had already, at his own cost, undertaken a certain amount of decoration recommended by the architect, proposed a plan to the Master for raising a distinct fund for the continuation of that work. He offered to be himself a further contributor of £50, on condition that nine other persons should give similar sums, within a given period. This proposition was warmly responded to; and before the end of the next month, the ten fifties were paid, or promised; besides some lesser sums for the same purpose. This fund has been applied specially to coloured ornamentation. Many friends, besides the pecuniary offerings, made themselves responsible for special portions of the work : such as stained glass windows, lectern, pulpit, communion-rail and carpet, sedilia, candle-standards, one hundred of the nave chairs, etc. The Hospital undertook the substantial oak stalling under the lantern.

The following summer did not pass without a further testimony on the part of "Z.O." of his continued interest in the work. He then offered his second benefaction in these terms, addressed to the Master :—

"9th July, 1866.

"Rev. Sir,—The writer offers to contribute the sum of £250 towards the expense of providing stained glass for St. Cross Church; and, assuming that, as yet, no steps have been taken to renew the west window, he would take the liberty of suggesting—

"1. That £200 be applied to the purpose of putting a new window at the west end of the church.

"2. That the remaining £50 be appropriated to the adaptation of the *ancient* glass now in the west window to windows in other parts of the church, and that on no account the old glass be removed from the church.

"3. That the modern glass now in the west window be excluded from that situation.

"4. That the firm of Messrs. Wailes, which he believes has already supplied some of the glass in the church, be engaged in this case.

"He hopes it will not be considered presuming to state that the above offer is made upon the understanding that the foregoing suggestions would be adopted, if they do not interfere with any plan that may have been already contemplated and approved."

"Z.O.'s" second donation was paid as promptly as his first. But a total sum of £500 is required to complete the proposed work: and, although Lord Eversley has promised £50, it is a matter for regret that sufficient money has not yet been raised to justify any step more active than preparing the plans; which Mr. Butterfield has undertaken to do.

In the course of the last year a substantial oak case was added to the organ, which had been before unprotected. During the present year, the Wandering Minstrels have most kindly given a second concert; which, after all expenses paid, has furnished one hundred pounds towards the requisite stall-work of the chancel. This important portion of the Church furniture, it is now hoped will be thoroughly and satisfactorily completed before Christmas; by which time, also, it is most earnestly to be desired that the west window fund may be sufficiently advanced for working purposes.

WHAT REMAINS TO BE DONE.

In the way of church restoration, several matters of more or less importance still require attention. For instance, the floor of the transepts has not yet been touched: it needs to be relaid after the fashion of the nave and aisles; especially the floor of the south transept. The groined chamber, contiguous to the south transept, might, with great advantage, be restored to what, we may assume, was its original purpose. It is wanted not only as a vestry, but as a kind of chapter room, or meeting place for the Master and brethren; particularly on more solemn occasions, such as the introduction and installation of a new member of the fraternity.

In the way of ornament, the elaborate stone screens, north and south of the chancel, call for attention. And additional stained glass might be inserted with great advantage; more especially in the nave.

For comfort, an additional Gurney-stove would be of great service for the more equal distribution of warmth. And, when opportunity offers, permanent seats for the nave, constructed with due regard to architectural effect, seem very desirable. The present chairs, which are excellent of their kind, will always be of important use for extra congregations and choral festivals.

It would not be difficult to enumerate other wants. The existing clock, after doing its duty well for a lengthened period of time, has of late been giving warning that its day of active usefulness is nearly over. It is of very ancient construction; and requiring to be wound up daily, has always been a source of some little anxiety and care to the aged brother whose duty it has been to preside over its destinies. A new clock, arranged to chime the quarters, as well as strike the hours, would be a vast improvement. The Master speaks the more feelingly on this point, because he has been writing this book within sound of such a clock, recently put up in the tower of the church which he has frequented, and in which he has spent many happy hours, during his unavoidable absence from home. The quarter-chimes, upon four bells, indicate the passage of time in the sweetest manner: and the voice of the chimes would tell its own appropriate lesson to the fraternity of St. Cross. The following lines, composed for St. Mark's, Brighton, are appended, with the kind permission of the writer :—

> Here for a time,
> Far off we roam ;
> Yet sings the chime,
> "Home, nearer Home."
> Sings through the night,
> Sings through the day,
> "Still fight the fight,
> Still watch and pray."
> Fast flies the time,
> Here overcome ;
> While sings the chime,
> Home ! nearer Home!

CONCLUSION.

It would have been easy to swell the catalogue of minor wants. The refectory needs greatly to be cleansed from whitewash and white paint, and made more suitable for its original use. But this, and other points, will be attended to in due season; when the Hospital has available funds, and is enabled to grapple, in some adequate degree, with the work before it. Till then, its progress can be but preliminary, and by instalments, as special circumstances, or the benevolence of individuals, enable it from time to time to anticipate its future.

With this conviction, the Master, though ready to avail himself to the utmost of any offer that may be volunteered for the benefit of his Church and Hospital, thinks that he has done enough in the way of public appeals. He is deeply sensible of the kindness with which such appeals have been hitherto received, and heartily thankful for the large measure of support which has been afforded to him from every side. He will carefully preserve what has been so far accomplished; and he will faithfully expend, to the best of his ability, whatever more may be intrusted to his charge. But his great object will be, as opportunity is given, to mature plans for the furtherance and extension of the Charity of which he is the guardian, and for the future development of its resources; knowing well, that the beauty of the Church, and even the order of its services, deeply important as those services are, form but a portion of the entire design which was planned by De Blois, and expanded by Beaufort.

That the benevolent schemes of these princely bishops and royal benefactors, so long and so often frustrated, may be, at length, as completely carried out, as their noble architecture is already to some extent restored; and that a far larger number of happy and united brethren may partake of their charity, and practically realise their pious wishes, by " humbly and devoutly serving God ;" is the earnest prayer of the writer of these pages, as, he trusts he may assume, it is also the sincere desire of the reader of them, and indeed of every one who has ever paid a visit to the pleasant and peaceful Hospital of the Holy Cross.

M

APPENDIX I.

RE-OPENING OF THE CHURCH OF ST. CROSS AT WINCHESTER.

THERE are few, probably, of the readers of the *John Bull* who do not feel an interest in the noble foundation of Henry de Blois, which adds another to the great glories of Winchester. Apart from the picturesque beauty and architectural importance of the buildings, the ancient character of the Institution, one of the few now left to us of its kind, with its common brotherhood, its religious garb, and its old form of hospitality, affords a link with ages gone by, which the Conservative character of our nation makes us cherish gratefully. Unfortunately, however, Conservatism has not always been discriminating as to what is worth preserving, and the Masters of St. Cross have, with the dole and the silver cross, tenaciously kept up other institutions of far more objectionable character. Thus, the Hospital archives record of one in the last century, that "he died three weeks after he had whitewashed the church." Mark, this is by no means to be regarded as a judgment on him; on the contrary, as memorial records are always framed upon the principle of *de mortuis nil nisi bonum*, it is rather to be construed as if he had added one more jewel to his crown, and so was ripe for departure. And when I last saw St. Cross, in the Exhibition year of 1851, that new era of light in art, the walls of the church had just received their periodical coating, at the especial command, as I was told, of the Master. Under the whitewash *régime*, then, the condition of Holy Cross Church had become rather discouraging, when the present enlightened Master first assumed the silver cross. The nave was a desert, the choir and sanctuary were blocked up with pews, dirt (save the whitewash), damp, and decay, reigned everywhere, and things probably would have been even worse, but for the archæological and historical interest attaching to the place, which brought it much under the notice of out-siders. Moreover, the most beautiful feature of the building, the east end, was disfigured by the zeal of a good Warden (*he* was no Conservative), who had blocked up the wonderful Norman windows with a perpendicular reredos. I forget his name, but he lies in the centre of the chancel, and the pleasure with which he must now contemplate the destruction of his handiwork will, I trust, compensate him for the purgatorial remorse he has suffered, since five centuries ago he must have found out what a blunder he had made. But I am anticipating.

It will be readily understood, then, that the new Master had no light work before him, in remedying the mistakes and shortcomings of his predecessors. His great difficulty has been to find the means. St. Cross has no repairing estate, and the Trustees have unluckily got into Chancery, which holds them pretty tight, so that they could do little. They made the nave decent, and restored the tower roof; they could do no more. And, overshadowed by the splendour of Winchester, St. Cross has not been able to establish its position as *the* county monument, and so draw into its meshes the county wealth, as Ely and Hereford have done.

An anonymous donor, who sent £500, gave a great impetus to the work. He made a condition that it should be spent upon the east end of the church; and the tiles of part of the choir, marked with "Z. O.," tell their eloquent tale of his modest devotion. Other sums soon came in, besides special gifts, and the result is a very grand, though incomplete, restoration. The great wonder is that so much has been done for the small sum of £2000, all raised as yet. For the whole of the church has been put in thorough good order. This implies a good deal, when the pew-encumbrance and the dilapidated floors are taken into consideration. Thus, the choir is properly filled with two rows of stalls for the brethren, and in lower grades seats for the choir. I pictured a goodly sight of the greyhaired, silver-crossed seniors in the stalls, and the double row of white-robed singers beneath them. But this picture was not realised. Next, the pavement has been relaid.

That in the choir and sanctuary, and up the centre of the nave is new, the rest is chiefly a collection of the old tiles, for which St. Cross was famous, carefully arranged, and, where necessary, completed by new work. Some Purbeck marble shafts have been introduced into the sanctuary, where a clean sweep has been made of the perpendicular reredos, and the result is an east wall of perfect Norman work of almost unique beauty. It is in three stages—the first contains two windows, with magnificent zigzag mouldings; the second, four, and the highest, two more. Much of the effect is due to a central pier which springs from the second stage to the groining of the roof. The glass of the windows represents, in the lower stage, the Nativity and the Epiphany (Old and New Christmas-Day—a happy juxtaposition); in the second, where the windows are necessarily narrow, some monograms; and in the higher stage the Resurrection and Ascension. But the rich effect here owes very much to the polychrome. I suppose that the strong colour of the lady who is said to symbolize the Papacy has brought about a confusion in people's minds. Certain it is that paint and Popery are by many regarded as synonymous. So that Mr. Butterfield's decorative project raised some alarm. But more formidable, because more reasonable, were the objections of those who thought that such rich architectural details would only be spoiled by any kind of addition. The result has, however, satisfied both classes of objectors. The Bishop, who is Visitor of the Hospital, not only gave his formal sanction to all the arrangements of the church and service, but expressed himself highly pleased with the polychrome. More-over, the Master on Thursday recorded the confessions of alarmists who admitted, some, that the east wall was innocent, others that it was not only innocent but effective. And the latter class of objectors were convinced (and admitted their convictions), by the instrumentality of their eyes, that colour, when judiciously applied, does not obscure, but brings out into greater prominence, elaborate architectural details. It is in this respect like a picture frame. The lower part of the east wall, Mr. Butterfield has filled in with a cross pattern of narrow tiles, permeated by a scroll pattern in black. In the upper stages the carving is judiciously picked out in colours, red predominating. Between the windows of the lower stage there is a cross in relief. I should say that all that has been done in this way hitherto, has been at the expense of Mr. Melville Portal, who wisely put his donation into this form. Other special gifts have been offered. Thus the lectern, a brass eagle, which cost £100, is a memorial.

The church was re-opened on Thursday, October 19th, A.D. 1865. The Bishop, who had been the guest of Sir William Heathcote, came over from Hursley Park, attended by Archdeacon Utterton and his Chaplains. He was met at the Master's house by the clergy, and went with them to the church. He was escorted to an imposing throne, set up for him in the sanctuary. The Bishop preached from Haggai ii, 9. He spoke warmly of the recovery of the church from its state of degradation and dishonour to something of its pristine glory. After the service was over, the old hall was filled with guests at the invitation of the Master. It was a scene of cheerful hospitality, such as had not been experienced within the walls for many a long year. There was abundance of decoration in the way of banners, boughs, and flowers, and plenty of good cheer. The Rt. Rev. Visitor presided, supported by the Master, who wore the silver cross of the brotherhood, and a number of influential residents in the diocese, the most conspicuous being Lord Eversley, Sir William Heathcote, Mr. Melville Portal, and Mr. Sclater-Booth, M.P. I wish that some of the lady choristers had taken their places in the "minstrels' gallery," this would have helped to bring the entertainment more in harmony with the scene of it. But what was wanting in music was supplied by eloquence. The Master gave "The Bishop" in a hearty genial speech. He reminded his lordship that he had never preached at St. Cross before, and prayed for a continuance of the favour. The Bishop's reply was kindness and geniality themselves, though he rather rated the county for not doing more for the work. He spoke very approvingly of the skill of Mr. Butterfield, the Architect, who unfortunately was obliged to go away before the luncheon. Lord Eversley, on behalf of the Trustees, was sorry that they could do so little for the work, but the grip of Chancery was so tight. Mr. Melville Portal returned thanks for the special donors, and thought that the Master was much too modest in asking for so small a sum as £2000. He ought to double his request. The Master had no objection to ask for £3000 more, especially as they had been obliged to put the Bishop into such a shabby pulpit that day, and moreover, as most of his hearers had learned experimentally, the church wanted a warming apparatus much.

None who attended on this interesting occasion could go away without feeling that a new era had been opened out for St. Cross, under the vigorous administration of Mr. Humbert, and the fostering care of the Visitor. But unless helped from without, the good work cannot be carried out as they wish. I do hope then that when pleasure or duty again takes me to that venerable hospice, I shall be able to tell how perfectly the Churchmen of Hampshire have restored St. Cross to its "pristine glory."—*Correspondent of John Bull.*

APPENDIX II.

THE CHURCH OF THE HOSPITAL OF ST. CROSS.

THE partial restoration of this beautiful fabric has already consumed, even under the most watchful economy, a sum approximately estimated at £2454. It is much to be regretted that the praiseworthy efforts, the persevering and commendable zeal of the Rev. the Master, has not yet met with more hearty sympathy and aid from every part of the diocese. This is more than a local church, and its claims should extend far and wide. It is one of the proudest monuments existing of a past age; for one may tread the length and breadth of this land, and yet no church would be found so interesting, beautiful and lofty in its proportions, and so worthy for those for whom it was built, who are none other than, in the beautiful and almost apostolic words of the Founder's Charter, "The Poor of Christ." The Hospital of St. Cross is the only Institution of its kind still existing, and perpetuates to this day the brotherhood system, so esteemed in the pre-Reformation era. Taking it altogether, both Church and Hospital present to the eye an unique and unrivalled memorial of the past. It still dispenses the charity of a pious Bishop of Winchester, who ruled the See no fewer than 700 years ago. For the credit of the county of Hants, and for the credit of the county of Surrey, and, indeed, for the sake of the entire Diocese, we hope that a more hearty response may yet be given to the appeal of the Right Rev. Prelate, who has so long and so worthily governed the Diocese, and has done so much to increase the comforts and position of his clergy, and for the advancement of education, so that the sum which yet remains to be collected, and is so urgently needed, for the completion and restoration of this large and beautiful church to its pristine state, with its enrichment and decorations, may be speedily forthcoming. For this purpose a sum perhaps as large as that which has been already expended is still required. Many windows, great and small, require glazing, the cost of which would vary from £25 to £35 each, and the gift of the glass for any of these windows would be a worthy and acceptable offering. We have not a doubt that these and other offerings will be made, and that the work so well begun will not be allowed to rest till it is satisfactorily completed.—*The Hampshire Chronicle.*

The Depot of City Memorials.

97, HIGH STREET, WINCHESTER.
A.D. m dccc xxxbi.

At this Establishment may be obtained Memorials of the Antient City for all purposes, ornamental and useful, which during the last thirty years have been designed by Mr. Savage, and made expressly for him by eminent Manufacturers in England, France, and Germany. The Articles are too numerous to particularize, but an idea of some at least may be gleaned from the above Photograph.

A DETAILED CATALOGUE POST FREE.

THE TRUSTY SERVANT, WINCHESTER COLLEGE.

SHORTLY WILL BE PUBLISHED

The Eighth Edition of Savage's Guide to the Antient City of Winchester, the College, St. Cross, and Hursley (the Home of Keble). This now well-known and favorite work is being revised and enlarged, and will soon be issued in a new and improved form, enriched according to the prevailing taste, and embellished with more than Thirty Engravings. The portion on the Home of Keble has been kindly undertaken by the Rev. J. Frewen Moor,* of Ampfield; while that on the Hospital of Saint Cross has been generously contributed by the Rev. L. M. Humbert, Master of Saint Cross.

Price in enamelled Wrapper, One Shilling; In Cloth elegant, Two Shillings.

* Author of Memorials of Reb. John Keble.

Memorials of the Rev. John Keble.

PUBLISHED BY MR. W. SAVAGE.

The Birthplace, Home, Churches, and other Places connected with the Author of "The Christian Year," illustrated in Thirty-two Photographs by W. Savage; with Memoir and Notes by the Rev. John Frewen Moor, jun., M.A. of Oriel College, Oxford. Winchester: W. Savage. London: James Parker & Co.

The memory and fame of the late Rev. John Keble, the author of "The Christian Year," will long remain enshrined in the hearts of all good men, and his devotional and heavenly lyrics be read and sung wherever true piety is to be found. The poetry of this distinguished scholar and divine is such as the Christian world will not willingly let die, and though their sainted author has passed away to his rest, and is now tuning his harp amidst the heavenly choir in even purer, higher, and holier strains than e'er he did on earth, he "being dead yet speaketh," and through the noble inheritance left behind him in "The Christian Year," and other works, will continue to elevate, instruct, and bless his countrymen and the world for generations to come.

The elegant and interesting volume now before us is a rich gallery of Biography, Poetry, and Art, commencing with a well written and exceedingly interesting Memoir of Mr. Keble, whose birth took place at Fairford, in Gloucestershire, on St. Mark's day, A.D. 1792. His father, the Rev. John Keble, vicar of Coln St. Aldwyn's, instructed him till he was in his fifteenth year, when he was sent to Oxford, where he at once distinguished himself, and obtained a scholarship; and four years later, at the Easter Term Examination, he gained the rare distinction of a "double first-class." Other fellowships, prizes, and academical honours rapidly followed, and in A.D. 1816 he was ordained deacon, and officiated as curate (in company with his brother) in two small churches, for which they received between them the liberal stipend of £65 per annum! Mr. Keble's poetic genius early manifested itself, and while very young he wrote some pieces of great beauty; but it was not till he was about twenty-seven years of age that he began to compose some of the hymns that afterwards resulted in that monument alike to his genius, his learning, and his piety—"The Christian Year." In A.D. 1827 he was induced, by the earnest pleadings of his friends, to publish the first edition of that noble book of Christian song, and the result has been that, while living, their distinguished author had the satisfaction of knowing that no fewer than ninety-two editions of the work was published in England, besides those in America, and elsewhere,—a tribute of homage to genius and piety rarely witnessed in the world of literature. Besides "The Christian Year," Mr. Keble was the author of many other Works, both in Poetry and Prose, amongst the former of which may be mentioned an edition of the Psalms in

MEMORIAL WINDOW
IN
AMPFIELD CHURCH.

verse. In August, A.D. 1836, he was instituted to the Vicarage of Hursley, with the Rectorship of Otterbourne, which had long been a curacy dependent on Hursley, though contributing the largest amount to the stipend of the Vicar of the latter place. In this calm retreat from the busy haunts of men, and employing his time in tending his spiritual flock like a "good shepherd," and in cultivating his refined and pious tastes as a scholar and a Christian poet, the Author of "The Christian Year" spent a long and peaceful lifetime, till a few months before his death, which took place at Bournemouth, on the 29th March, A.D. 1866. His remains were interred in Hursley Churchyard on 6th April, and the "clouds of the valley" closed over all that was mortal of this sainted son of sacred song.

Scattered throughout this superb volume, we have many extracts from Mr. Keble's poetical productions, "like orient pearls at random strung," and which describe and illustrate many of the scenes and places connected with the worthy pastor's life and labours. Along with these literary gems, we have some artistic ones of rare beauty, one of the finest of which—a wood engraving—is the ruins of the "Chancel of the old church at Otterbourne." But the book is essentially and profusely illustrated by photographs, which—thirty-two in number—thickly intersect the literary portion of the work, and reproduce with great fidelity almost every place which, in any way, in early or later life, had any connection with the Author of "The Christian Year." We have, first, a portrait of the distinguished Bard, then Fairford, the Poet's birthplace, Fairford Church; Corpus Christi College and Oriel College, Oxford; and many other Churches, amongst which may be mentioned Hursley Church, Church-yard, and Vicarage; Otterbourne Church and Otterbourne Parsonage; Ampfield Church and Ampfield Parsonage; and the Graves of Mr. and Mrs. Keble, where—

> "Amid the swelling mounds that told,
> Where dust to kindred dust was laid,
> Two grassy hillocks side by side,
> With kindling interest are surveyed."

These "Memorials of the Rev. John Keble" are beautifully printed in toned paper, with Oxford border to every page, and apart from their intrinsic merits as a loving record to the memory of a good and great man, are worthy of a place in any drawing room, from the handsome manner in which the work has been got up.—*The Shields Times.*

Price—In Cloth elegant, £2 : 2 : 0; in Morocco, very rich, same style as the Queen's copy. £4 : 4 : 0.